THE SUN CATCHERS
HUMMINGBIRDS

Anna's Hummingbird

NorthWord

WILDLIFE SERIES

DEDICATION

In loving memory of my mother,
who taught me to find joy in little things.
—J. P. S.

ACKNOWLEDGMENTS

We are deeply indebted to the many authors whose papers, books, and articles illuminate hummingbird behavior and ecology. To these dedicated researchers, naturalists, and educators, we offer our sincerest thanks for the help they have given us and so many others over the years.

Special thanks go out to the people who reviewed all or part of our manuscript: Dr. Lee Gass at the University of British Columbia; Dr. Frank Gill at the Academy of Natural Sciences in Philadelphia; Karen Krebbs, Assistant Curator at the Arizona–Sonora Desert Museum; Dr. Don Powers at George Fox College; Dr. Peter Scott at Indiana State University; and Sheri Williamson and Tom Wood at Ramsey Canyon Preserve. Additional thanks to Sheri Williamson for reviewing all the photos.

We are also thankful for the following researchers who took time out of their busy schedules to answer questions: Dr. Bill Baltosser; Dr. Bill Calder, III; and Dr. Steve Russell. Thanks also to Freda Kinoshita and René Corado of the Western Foundation of Vertebrate Biology and Cindy Lippincott at the American Birding Association.

The efforts of these people certainly improved the quality of this book. Any errors that remain are our responsibility, not due to their sincere efforts to steer us in the right direction.

Blue-throated Hummingbird

Photographs © 1996: Rick & Nora Bowers, Front Cover, 15, 16, 58, 77, 108, 124, 134; Hugh P. Smith Jr., 1, 30-31, 55, 86, 92-93, 104, 140-141; Bob & Clara Calhoun/Bruce Coleman, Inc., 2-3, 8, 34, 46, 53, 56, 66, 84, 97, 98, 106, 110, 112, 122, 126; Clayton A. Fogle, 6-7, 44-45; G. C. Kelley/Tom Stack & Associates, 11, 23, 114; Charles Melton/The Wildlife Collection, 18-19, 28, 60, 72, 95, 118, 130, 132; Art Wolfe, 20; E. R. Degginger/Bruce Coleman, Inc., 24; Robert Lankinen/The Wildlife Collection, 26-27, 128; David L. Sladky, 32-33; Anthony Mercieca/Dembinsky Photo Associates, 37, 50-51, 70, 116, Back Cover; Wayne Lankinen/Bruce Coleman, Inc., 41; Richard Hamilton Smith, 42-43, 89; Dan Dempster/Dembinsky Photo Associates, 48-49; John H. Hoffman/Bruce Coleman, Inc., 63; Francois Gohier, 64-65, 68, 82; Tom & Pat Leeson, 74; Roger Eriksson, 78, 80-81; Richard Day/Daybreak Imagery, 101; Jeff Foott/Bruce Coleman, Inc., 102-103; Alan G. Nelson/Dembinsky Photo Associates, 120.

NorthWord Press, Inc.
P.O. Box 1360
Minocqua, WI 54548

Book design by Lisa Moore

For a free catalog describing our audio products, nature books and calendars, call **1-800-356-4465**, or write Consumer Inquiries, NorthWord Press, Inc., P.O. Box 1360, Minocqua, Wisconsin 54548

Library of Congress Cataloging-in-Publication Data
Sayre, Jeff
      Hummingbirds : the sun catchers / by Jeff Sayre and April
Pulley Sayre.
         p.   cm.—(Wildlife series)
      Includes bibliographical references.
      ISBN 1-55971-571-5 (sc)
      1. Hummingbirds—North America. I. Sayre, April Pulley. II. Title.
III. Series: Wildlife series
QL696.A558S28 1996
598.8'99—dc20   96-11584

Printed in Singapore

THE SUN CATCHERS
HUMMINGBIRDS

by Jeff and April Sayre

NorthWord

NORTHWORD PRESS, INC.
Minocqua, Wisconsin

Broad-tailed and Rufous Hummingbirds

$\mathscr{C}$ONTENTS

Anna's Hummingbird

Even as we begin writing this book, we are surrounded by hummingbirds. A Broad-billed Hummingbird, clothed in purple, sits on a nearby branch. A Costa's Hummingbird turns its head toward the sun and ignites with color. A Lucifer uses its delicate, curved bill to probe a trumpet-shaped bloom. And one curious female Anna's Hummingbird keeps moving closer.

"She's right behind you," whispers my husband Jeff. I already know. A gentle breeze made by her wings ruffles my hair. Her feathers quietly hum. As she moves away, then back, the breeze comes and goes. Most likely, the hummingbird is simply catching gnats flying close to my head, but her visit seems like a gift, nonetheless. We never cease to marvel at these strange little birds: their shimmering colors and their acrobatic flight. The more we learn about their ecological relationships with flowers, spiders, woodpeckers and even mites, the more we appreciate them.

Plip! . . . the Anna's has just deposited a clear, wet dropping on the paragraph I just wrote. Is that an opinion? One can only speculate. She quickly whirs away.

Encounters With Hummingbirds

Our encounter with the Anna's Hummingbird took place in the Hummingbird House of the Arizona–Sonora Desert Museum. But you can find hummingbirds all over North and South America. They are uniquely American—only inhabiting North America, Central America, South America, and islands nearby. Other continents have nectar-feeding birds: the sunbirds of Africa and Asia and the honeyeaters of Australia. But these birds are not closely related to hummingbirds. Hummingbirds, in their supremely acrobatic flight, their species diversity, and their close relationships with flowers and pollination, surpass these other nectar feeders, in many people's opinion.

Long, slender bills, short legs, and a unique method of flight are among the hallmarks of the hummingbird clan. Scientifically speaking, hummingbirds belong to the family Trochilidae. Their closest avian relatives are the swifts. Swifts, however, don't fly like hummingbirds. Hummingbirds' short, stiff wings beat the air, and twist in a figure eight pattern while hovering. Hummingbirds are the helicopters of the avian world: the most maneuverable of all birds. Not only can hummingbirds hover and fly backward, they can even briefly fly upside down. Other birds, in contrast, flex and bend their wings as they flap. This uses less energy, but prevents them from changing direction as quickly as hummingbirds.

Range

Worldwide, there are 341 hummingbird species, give or take a few, depending on which expert you consult. Of these, sixteen nest in North America. (Although continental North America includes Mexico, Central America, and the West Indies, this book will use the term "North America" only in reference to Canada and the United States.) The nesting hummingbirds of North America include: Allen's, Anna's, Berylline, Black-chinned, Blue-throated, Broad-billed, Broad-tailed, Buff-bellied, Calliope, Costa's, Lucifer, Magnificent, Ruby-throated, Rufous, Violet-crowned and White-eared. An additional ten species have visited but are not known to have nested in the continental United States. These include: Antillean Crested, Bahama Woodstar, Bumblebee, Cinnamon, Cuban Emerald, Green Violet-ear, Green-breasted Mango, Plain-capped Starthroat, Rufous-tailed and Xantus'. A female Xantus' did nest in California but unsuccessfully. Again, how many visiting birds you count depends on whose accounts you believe. The fact

Magnificent Hummingbird

remains: hummingbirds are incredibly diverse. In the western hemisphere, the hummingbird family is the second largest, after flycatchers, which number 367 species.

Hummingbirds range widely in the Americas. One cold day in Alaska, after walking near Portage glacier, we stopped to eat lunch at a restaurant. We were shocked to see hummingbird feeders hanging outside all the windows. At that time, we could not imagine hummingbirds living in such a cold climate. But as we ate, a hummingbird came to the feeder right outside the window. It was our first sight of a gorgeous Rufous Hummingbird.

As we later discovered, hummingbirds live all the way from Alaska to Tierra Del Fuego at the southern tip of South America. They also range onto islands, such as those in the Caribbean and the Juan Fernandez islands west of Chile. In 1976, one wayward Rufous Hummingbird reportedly even made its way to Ratmanov Island, a former Soviet holding in the Bering Strait.

Biologists have discovered that the number of plant and animal species increases near the equator and decreases toward the poles. The same is true of hummingbird species. The greatest diversity is found in the tropics. Ecuador has 163 hummingbird species, more than ten times as many as nest in the continental United States. Canada, which is farther from the equator, has only five nesting hummingbird species.

Surprisingly adaptable, hummingbirds seem to live wherever there is nectar to drink and insects to catch. They range from low altitudes near seashores to high altitudes on mountaintops. Some live as high as 16,500 feet above sea level, where oxygen is relatively scarce and people can become altitude sick. In fact, hummingbirds make up a large percentage of the bird life on many tropical mountaintops.

Although hummingbirds do nest in such chilly locales, many migrate to avoid the coldest parts of the year. North American hummingbirds, except Anna's and some populations of Allen's and Costa's, migrate south in the winter. The Rufous we saw in Alaska, for instance, will not stay for the dark, cold winter. Blooming flowers are nonexistent and insects hibernate during the long Arctic winters. With those tiny wings, some Rufous Hummingbirds make a stupendous journey of over two thousand miles, all the way to Mexico. Some Calliope Hummingbirds fly even farther, about 2,790 miles. If you compare how far it travels with how big it is, the Calliope makes the longest journey of any bird on earth.

Ruby-throated Hummingbirds, common in the eastern United States, are also migratory; they travel to Central America in winter. During their migration, many Ruby-throated Hummingbirds fly from the southeastern United States across the five hundred-mile-wide Gulf of Mexico. The task is arduous.

Rumors that hummingbirds fly across the Gulf of Mexico by hitching rides on the backs of larger birds is unsupported by even a shred of solid evidence. But it makes such a great story, we almost wish it were true!

However, there's no need to make up unbelievable stories about hummingbirds. Their real biology and behavior is mind-boggling enough. By most estimates, hummingbirds are some of the smallest warm-blooded animals on earth. They have the fastest wingbeat of any bird. They have the largest heart relative to their body size. And they hatch from the smallest bird egg—some smaller than a pea.

Names

The problem with trying to describe hummingbirds is that the best adjectives are already taken as hummingbird names. You could say they're magnificent. But there is already a species, the Magnificent Hummingbird, in North America. A genus of hummingbirds is called Brilliant, by name. A whole host of gems, minerals, flowers, flames, and even planets crop up in hummingbird names. Consider some of the names of these hummingbird species: Green-breasted Mango, Fiery-tailed Awlbill, Crowned Woodnymph, Esmerelda Woodstar, Flame-rumped Sapphire, Glittering-throated Emerald, Bronze-tailed Plumeleteer, Blossomcrown, Bearded Helmetcrest, Red-tailed Comet, Rainbow Starfrontlet, Tourmaline Sunangel, Andean Hillstar, Horned Sungem and Hooded Visorbearer.

Even the scientific names of hummingbirds are unusually steeped in poetry. The genus that includes North America's Rufous and Allen's hummingbirds is *Selasphorous*, from Greek words meaning "light" and "bearing." Other genera include: *Heliodoxa*—"sun glory," *Hylocharis*—"beauty of the forest" and *Stellula*—"little star."

In other languages, the common terms for hummingbirds reflect their beauty and behavior as well. The Creole term is *murmures*—"the murmurers." In Brazil, they have the romantic Portuguese name of *beija flor*—"the flower kissers." In Mexico, they are *chuparosas*—the "rose suckers." A friend of ours from central Mexico says people in her town call the birds "coquettes." A scientific genus of hummingbirds also goes by the name *coquette*.

Folklore

Hummingbirds' fiery natures and beautiful feathers play a part in the folklore and customs of many cultures. Centuries ago, the ceremonial cloaks of the Aztecs were adorned with hummingbird feathers. Europeans' love affair with hummingbirds did not come into full swing until the mid- to late-1800s, when trade with the Americas was well-established. Unfortunately, Europeans' adoration proved less than beneficial for the birds. Hundreds of thousands of hummingbirds were killed in South America and exported to Europe and the United States, where the stuffed birds were displayed in private collections and even on ladies' hats. The feathers were also used to decorate paintings, fans, and shoes. Records show as many as twelve thousand hummingbird skins were sold in one month in London.

Even today, dried, powdered hummingbirds are sold in Mexico as a kind of "love medicine." The powder, incorporated into soap, becomes a love soap, with which people bathe in order to attract the right man or woman. In Mexican markets, dead hummingbirds are sold as portable love charms as well.

Fortunately, these days, most people express their admiration for hummingbirds not by wearing the birds themselves, but by wearing paintings of them instead. It seems every imaginable product, from T-shirts, mugs, tables, scarves, earrings and necklaces to hats are emblazoned with hummingbirds. People are also putting up feeders to attract them. They're planting hummingbird gardens, full of flowers that provide nectar for the birds. Hummingbird enthusiasts even gather each year at a week-long hummingbird festival in Texas to exchange information and anecdotes and revel in their love of hummingbirds.

Perhaps that's as it should be. There's much to admire about these colorful, vibrant birds. As Roger Tory Peterson says, "Birds have to be one of the most vivid expressions of life there is." For many people, the hovering, sparkling, hummingbirds are an especially appropriate embodiment of motion, energy, and life.

Anna's Hummingbird

Broad-billed Hummingbird

Visiting hummingbird feeders in the backyards of people you don't know may seem like a strange thing to do. But in several places in southeastern Arizona, it is socially acceptable, and often encouraged. A few generous people maintain large numbers of feeders and open their yards to bird watchers who want to view the birds. Crowds can gather—sometimes forty people—plus a hundred or more hummingbirds. Then a strange phenomenon occurs: people periodically break out in choruses of "oohs" and "aahs" as if they were watching a fireworks display. Chances are, even if you are a reserved and quiet birder, you will soon find yourself "oohing" and "aahing" with the rest, enchanted by the spectacular show of hummingbirds.

A Rainbow of Color

Part of the drama of watching hummingbirds is that they appear strikingly different in different light. Like a sequined dress, a hummingbird's feathers may look dark in some lights, and shine brightly in others. A crowd of hummingbirds around a partly-shaded hummingbird feeder can appear dark and uniform

in color, even if several species are actually present. Yet when a humming-bird, for instance a male Calliope, turns and faces the sun, its head and throat feathers blaze with red. In a crowd of bird watchers, the sight of these colors can cause a contagious chain reaction, a gasp that spreads from one individual to the next. Few are unmoved by the sight.

The brilliant feathers that cause this transformation are called iridescent feathers, for the peculiar way they sparkle in the light. Highly iridescent feathers may adorn a hummingbird's head or, like a snappy scarf, shine on its gorget—its throat and chin. With the exception of flight feathers, all the feathers of a hummingbird usually show some degree of iridescence. In some species, flight feathers may be slightly iridescent too.

Although pigments create the rufous color in hummingbirds, pigments are not responsible for the brilliant blues, reds, purples, and greens of iridescent feathers. These are "structural colors," created by specialized feathers that contain between seven and fifteen layers of pancake-shaped platelets. Each platelet is filled with air pockets. When light strikes the platelets, it is reflected back. Depending on the thickness of the platelets and the size of the air pockets, a specific wavelength of light is reflected back. Thicker platelets reflect light in the red range of the spectrum while thinner platelets reflect blue. The more layers, the more intense the reflected light.

A hummingbird's gorget appears to glow only when viewed from head-on, with the light source at the viewer's back. The flat shape of most gorget feathers reflect light only in one direction. When seen from any other angle, the feathers appear dull brown to black. The other iridescent feathers have concave platelets, which create less spectacular color but can reflect light from any angle. These feathers appear green or light blue.

Scientists believe the different intensities of feather iridescence may be adaptive in several ways. The most brilliant and conspicuous feathers, those of the gorget, are difficult to see except at the right angle. This makes it harder for a potential predator to locate an unsuspecting hummingbird. Yet these feathers can still be flashed for territorial and courtship displays. The other iridescent feathers always shine. But they do not glow as intensely and are greenish in hue, so they may help the hummingbird blend with the green foliage of plants.

Preceding page: Violet-crowned Hummingbird

Left: Calliope Hummingbird

Blueprint for Takeoff

With the exception of bats, birds are the only warm-blooded animals that can truly fly. A bird's skeletal system is composed of very light, hollow bones, many of which contain internal struts. Although it may seem that such a light structure would not provide much strength, bird bones actually are remarkably strong for their weight. If a bird's bones were solid, like those of most terrestrial vertebrates, the bird would weigh too much to fly efficiently, if at all.

As with all birds, a hummingbird's wing bones are modified versions of the upper arm, forearm and hand. The wing bones of hummingbirds, however, have different relative dimensions than those of other birds. Most birds have long upper arm bones and forearm bones, and short hand bones. Hummingbirds have very short upper arms and forearms but considerably longer hand bones. Because of this unusual arrangement, a hummingbird's wings are not able to flex like those of other birds.

Another interesting feature of a bird's skeleton is the breast bone, or sternum. Birds that fly have an enlarged sternum which contains a keel—a bony projection similar to its nautical namesake. Flightless birds, such as Emus, Ostriches and Kiwis, do not have a keeled sternum. A bird's flying ability is related to the size of its keel. The larger or longer the keel, the more adept a bird is at flying. Proportionately, hummingbirds have the largest and longest keel of any bird family. This provides more space for the attachment of a hummingbird's relatively large, powerful flight muscles.

Attached to the keel are the main flight muscles. One, the pectoral muscle, pulls the wing down on what is called the power stroke. The other, which has the tongue-tangling name of supracoracoideus, pulls the wing up on the recovery stroke. In most birds that fly, the pectoral muscle and associated muscles are much larger than the supracoracoideus muscles and account for about fifteen percent of the weight of the bird. But in hummingbirds, both these muscle groups are large. Depending on the species, they may make up thirty-five percent of the weight of the bird. The advantage of such a large supracoracoideus muscle is that it enables the upstroke of the wings to act as a power stroke that propels the bird, instead of just a recovery stroke.

A hummingbird's mode of flight and rapid metabolism require an efficient circulatory and respiratory system. It's not surprising, then, that relative to all animals, hummingbirds have the largest heart. At rest, their hearts beat about five hundred times per minute. When excited, such as during courtship or when chasing off an intruder, the rate can jump to 1,200 beats per minute.

Broad-billed Hummingbird

The way birds breathe is even more remarkable. Among vertebrates, birds have the greatest oxygen demand. To meet this demand, birds not only have two compact, spongy lungs, but also a system of air sacs. Air sacs are basically extensions of the lungs. They surround and protect internal organs and even extend into the wings and legs. The number of air sacs varies among bird families. Most, such as the hummingbird family, have nine; but others have as few as six or as many as twelve.

Unlike mammals, birds have a respiratory system that is very efficient, making possible a continuous, unidirectional flow of air through the lungs.

Broad-billed Hummingbird

The lungs, air sacs and one-way air flow enable large quantities of oxygen to be delivered throughout the body. The system also plays another vital role: helping remove life-threatening body heat generated during flight. An added benefit is that because of the efficiency of the avian respiratory system, living or flying in oxygen-depleted high altitudes is of little problem for most birds.

Feathers to Flight

A bird's bone structure, muscles, circulatory system, and respiratory system are integral parts of an overall system that enable them to exploit the air. But without feathers, they would not get very far. Feathers are unique structures in the animal world. Only birds have feathers, and all birds have them. Scientists believe that as birds evolved from reptiles (some current theories hold that birds are living dinosaurs), feathers evolved from scales. However, the chemical composition of feathers is markedly different from that of reptilian scales.

Feathers are remarkably strong, durable, lightweight and flexible. They insulate birds, help them to fly, and give them their streamlined appearance. Feathers fall into many categories. The main ones include: contour feathers, down feathers and flight feathers. Contour feathers are the basic body feathers: the small, visible feathers that coat the body, as opposed to long flight feathers of the wings and tail. Down feathers are fluffy feathers that keep birds warm and may be tucked underneath contour feathers. Young birds often grow a whole coat of downy feathers, but hummingbirds just have a few scraggly ones at birth.

Flight feathers are longer, larger, and different in structure from the contour feathers and downy feathers, and are responsible for providing lift, thrust and balance during flight. The flight feathers of the wings are further divided into two groups: the primaries and the secondaries. Primaries, which provide the forward thrust of flight, are the outermost flight feathers and attach to the bones of the hand. Hummingbirds, like most other birds, have ten primaries. The secondaries, the feathers responsible for generating lift, are attached to the bones of the forearm. Hummingbirds usually have only six secondaries, the fewest in the avian world.

The total mass of feathers on a bird weighs two to three times as much as its bones. On average, hummingbirds have roughly 1,500 feathers, in contrast to Tundra Swans, which have 25,000 feathers, and songbirds which have about 2,000 to 4,000. Hummingbirds, although they have fewer feathers, have small bodies, so their feathers are tightly packed. A hummingbird has more feathers per square centimeter than any other bird.

Masters of the Air

Among hummingbirds, maximum flight speed and wingbeat depend on the size and weight of the hummingbird, the length of its wings, and the velocity of the wind. In general, smaller hummingbirds have faster wingbeats than larger ones. The tiny Amethyst Woodstar, a bird of the tropics, beats its wings about eighty times per second. The wingbeat of the Giant Hummingbird of the high Andes ranges from about ten to fifteen beats per second. Rufous and Ruby-throated Hummingbirds, however, may reach the phenomenal wingbeat rate of almost two hundred beats per second during courtship dives!

Accurate data on how fast hummingbirds fly is somewhat limited. The most accurate measures of a Ruby-throated Hummingbird, taken in the controlled environment of a wind tunnel, established a flight speed of about 27 mph.

When seen on slow-motion film, the wings of an Arctic Tern

flex as they flap, with a graceful motion like a ballet dancer's arms. Hummingbirds, in contrast, do not flex their wings at the wrist or elbow joint in flight, as do most other birds. A hummingbird's wings move with short, stiff, oar-like motions, at times rotating almost 180 degrees at the shoulder joint. This stiff wing motion gives hummingbirds a power advantage. Most birds generate power only on the downstroke of their wing beat; yet due to the unique structure of their wings, hummingbirds generate power on the upstroke too.

Hummingbirds can change direction almost instantly. By tilting the plane of their wings, they can control with great precision how fast and in which direction they fly. During forward movement, the wingtips trace a

Rufous Hummingbird

vertical oval in the air. During backward movement, they trace a horizontal oval slightly above the bird. While hovering, the wingtips trace a figure eight, with one loop larger than the other. The figure eight lies parallel to the plane of level ground. Hummingbirds are also capable of brief periods of upside-down flight when startled.

Hummingbirds may be the masters of acrobatic flight. But the size and shape of their wings, combined with the energy required to power their large flight muscles, makes their mode of flight among the most inefficient in the avian world. Their hovering, flitting and diving comes at a great cost, requiring the birds to constantly seek food to provide them with energy.

Anna's Hummingbird

Great Migrations

Twice each year in North America, over five billion individual birds of two hundred different species make a long and dangerous journey: they migrate. In the spring, the birds travel to their breeding grounds in the temperate north; in fall they return to their wintering grounds in the tropics.

Most, but not all, North American hummingbirds are migratory. Ruby-throated Hummingbirds fly from their summer homes in eastern North America to wintering grounds in Mexico and Central America. Another famous migrant is the Rufous Hummingbird. Some Rufous Hummingbirds fly over two thousand miles from Alaska to Mexico.

Anna's Hummingbirds are year-round residents of the West Coast, and one subspecies of the Allen's Hummingbird is a year-long resident of the Channel Islands off the southern coast of California and the Palos Verdes Peninsula. Also, some Costa's Hummingbirds are year-round residents in southern California and southwestern Arizona.

The evolutionary origins of hummingbird migration are still a puzzle. But scientists agree that two of the basic advantages migration offers are favorable climates and food resources throughout the year. In tropical regions, the number of hours of daylight is almost unchanging year-round, and temperatures are fairly constant. But competition for food and nesting sites is fierce. By spending spring and summer in temperate regions, migrants benefit from the longer period of daylight, abundant food supplies and numerous nesting sites. In fall, when the hours of the daylight decrease, temperatures drop and food becomes scarce, migrants leave for places more accommodating—places farther south, such as the tropics.

It is difficult enough for a small warbler to successfully complete a long migratory journey, but at one-fourth its size and with its high metabolism, a hummingbird faces even more of a challenge. Unlike most birds, hummingbirds, at least some species, may migrate during the day. According to scientists, over fifty percent of migratory birds never return to their summer breeding sites; they die either en route or on their wintering grounds. Nevertheless, migratory hummingbirds still manage to succeed. After a journey of thousands of miles and after a period of seven months, tiny hummingbirds can still find their way back to the same nest site in the very same tree.

One of the keys to hummingbirds' success is the buildup of sufficient fat reserves to fuel their migratory flights. During migration, hummingbirds make frequent refueling stops, spending a week or more at a stopover to replenish and add to their fat reserves. Some species of hummingbirds set up temporary territories during their stopovers. Ruby-throated Hummingbirds, which make long, non-stop migratory flights over the waters of the Gulf of Mexico, may put on as much as two grams of fat in preparation for the journey. This amount of fat represents a gain of almost two-thirds of a Ruby-throated Hummingbird's body weight.

In the late winter and early spring, most returning hummingbirds in western North America migrate through the lower elevations of the Pacific slope and Colorado plateau. During this time of year, it is in those areas that flowers are blooming. However, in the late summer and fall, most flowers have stopped blooming in the valley lowlands. So, in the post-breeding season, many

hummingbirds that breed at lower elevations move to higher elevations to feed on alpine wildflowers that are then in bloom.

Hummingbirds heading south for the winter concentrate in these higher altitudes, following the late summer bloom and fattening up for their long journeys. Commonly, the males start their migration before the juvenile hummingbirds have left the nest. Some researchers speculate that this behavior is an evolutionary adaptation that reduces the competition for food with female and immature hummingbirds that must also fatten up for their long migrations.

Bathing And Preening

Iridescent feathers are not as showy and flight feathers are not as functional if they are grimy. Hummingbirds bathe by fluttering their wings among leaves wetted by dew or rain. They shake and flutter in a light rain, or the spray of a waterfall, a sprinkler or a hose. After a bath, and many other times throughout the day, hummingbirds preen.

Preening is the fluffing, straightening and oiling required for daily feather maintenance. As feathers get old, they become dry and brittle if not cared for properly. Most birds, including hummingbirds, have a uropygial gland, located underneath the base of their tail. This gland secretes a waxy polish. With their bills, hummingbirds gather a bit of the polish and apply it to their feathers. The oily, waxy material from the gland also helps inhibit the growth of fungi and bacteria that damage feathers. While preening, hummingbirds not only spread this oil, they also smooth ruffled feathers by running their bills along the shafts. They pick out parasites lodged among feathers and generally clean themselves off. Their feet come in handy too—for reaching up and scratching itchy places and cleaning sticky nectar and sap off the bill.

Anna's Hummingbird

Out With the Old

Feathers are made of durable protein. But even with proper maintenance, the stresses of flight, weather, and midair battles can take its toll as the season progresses. Edges fray and wear down. Feathers can be severely damaged or even lost. To counter this effect, all birds undergo a molt—a shedding and regrowth of feathers—at least once a year. In general, a full molt of all body feathers occurs when migratory hummingbirds are on their wintering grounds.

Hummingbirds don't molt all their feathers at once; otherwise we'd see naked hummingbirds streaking around. Instead, like other birds, hummingbirds shed feathers a few at a time. Underneath the old feathers, new feathers form. These feathers are encased in the translucent white shaft of the old feather's quill. As the new feather emerges, it actually pushes the old feather

Ruby-throated Hummingbird

out. When a feather on one side of the bird is being shed, the corresponding one on the other side is shed as well. Molting begins with the primaries followed by the secondaries, the tail feathers and then the contour feathers. But within these categories, feathers are shed in varying orders, according to the molting pattern of that particular hummingbird species. The contour feathers are replaced starting at the tail-end of the bird and moving up to the head.

Interestingly, although hummingbirds begin a molt on their wintering grounds, the feathers of the head and gorget are usually not replaced until close to breeding season. That way the bird has fresh feathers ready for the showy displays required to defend a territory and attract a mate.

Broad-billed Hummingbird

DIET FOR A HIGH-ENERGY BIRD

Fast-flying hummingbirds burn up energy like race cars burn gas. So, to power their internal "engines," hummingbirds feed on an energy-rich food: flower nectar. For hummingbirds, nectar is an almost perfect food—easy to digest, and quickly converted to energy. That's important because hummingbirds burn a tremendous number of calories even when quietly perching. To fuel a typical day of flitting, hovering, darting, fighting and other activities, a hummingbird must consume the nectar of more than a thousand flowers.

To feed, a hummingbird hovers in front or below a flower, thrusting its long bill into the tubular blossom until it locates the nectar. Popular myth has it that hummingbirds suck nectar through a straw-like bill. This is untrue. Instead, a hummingbird uses its forked tongue to lap nectar at a rate of between eight and twelve laps per second, depending on species and nectar viscosity. Feeding five to ten times an hour is not unusual. Between feedings, and when not defending a territory, hummingbirds perch and rest to conserve energy. By the end of a long day, zipping from flower to flower, a hummingbird may have consumed one-and-a-half to three times its body weight in nectar.

Hummingbird Foods: Beyond Nectar

Carbohydrate-rich nectar is a good energy source. But hummingbirds still need a balanced diet, including protein, vitamins, minerals, fat and water. Although a few hummingbird flowers provide nectar with amino acids that meet some of these needs, the largest sources of protein for hummingbirds are insects and spiders. Early attempts at raising hummingbirds in captivity failed due to the lack of protein in their diet. Their captors didn't realize that such graceful, petite, sugar-lapping birds were also voracious meat-eaters.

Part of a hummingbird's time is spent searching for insects and small spiders on flowers, under leaves, or in the air. Some hummingbirds even gather insects by snatching them from spiderwebs! When nectar sources dry up, hummingbirds spend almost all of their foraging time hunting insects.

Water, too, is a dietary necessity. Each day, hummingbirds consume many times as much water as they do solid food. They obtain most of their water from nectar, but may also drink water from natural springs, streams, birdbaths and fountains.

Water probably does more than quench a hummingbird's thirst. A hummingbird spends so much time sticking its bill and face into flowers that the sugary, sticky nectar coats its bill and facial feathers. Some scientists believe frequent forays to a water source may help free up sticky feathers and dissolve sugar coatings on a hummingbird's bill.

Tree sap is also a popular hummingbird food. Sap has a sugar content close to that of flower nectar. Of course, a hummingbird's bill isn't fit for drilling holes in tree bark to get the sap. Instead, hummingbirds drink sap from holes made by sapsuckers—woodpeckers that drill holes in trees.

In North America, the Ruby-throated, Calliope, Broad-tailed, Blue-throated and Rufous Hummingbirds have learned to exploit this extra food source. They follow sapsuckers, such as Yellow-bellied Sapsuckers or Red-naped Sapsuckers around the forest. (One obviously confused hummingbird was spotted following a Hairy Woodpecker, a species which does not drill for sap.) Some hummingbirds learn the locations of the holes and return to them. Rufous Hummingbirds even set up territories to protect their sapsucker holes.

For at least two species, the Ruby-throated Hummingbird and the Rufous Hummingbird, sapsucker holes seem essential for survival. Ruby-throated Hummingbirds return north from their wintering grounds in Central America several weeks before the flowers they feed upon bloom. If they didn't have an alternative source of food, they would likely perish. Research has shown that Ruby-throated Hummingbirds rely on insects and sap to sustain them until the flowers bloom. This is also the case with Rufous Hummingbirds. Remarkably, the northernmost range of both the Ruby-throated and Rufous Hummingbirds appears to be controlled more by the range of the sapsuckers than by flower availability.

Rufous Hummingbird

Small Birds, Big Appetites

Hummingbirds have among their ranks what is probably the smallest warm-blooded creature on earth: the Cuban Bee Hummingbird. It measures 2-1/4 inches from bill-tip to tail-tip, and weighs less than a penny.

Small body size, however, does not mean a small appetite. Although tiny, hummingbirds can eat up to three-fourths their body weight in sugar every day. To meet its daily energy needs, an Anna's Hummingbird must consume between 7.6 and 10.3 Calories per day. That may not seem like much compared to the average adult human's intake of 1,500 to 3,500 Calories per day. But for a hummingbird, 10 Calories is actually a phenomenal amount. A human being with a comparable metabolism to an Anna's Hummingbird would require 165,000 Calories in food per day to keep from starving. That's like consuming 3,500 pancakes each day, or eating approximately one five-pound bag of table sugar every forty minutes while you're awake! Fortunately for us, we have more modest energy needs than hummingbirds do.

The key to hummingbirds' big appetites is their high metabolic rate. The Cuban Bee Hummingbird probably has the highest metabolic rate of *any* warm-blooded animal. The reason small warm-blooded animals have high metabolic rates is that they face physiological challenges that larger animals do not.

The smaller the animal, the more surface area it has compared to its volume. The greater the surface area, the faster heat is lost to the environment. In order to counteract this loss, small-bodied animals must have a much higher metabolic rate than larger ones, just to churn out enough heat to stay warm. Consequently, relative to their body size, small animals must eat more food than larger animals do. And what makes the problem more severe is that, with the exception of a few migratory species, hummingbirds do not have a sufficient reserve of fat to use in lean times. So, for a hummingbird, one unsuccessful day of foraging could literally mean its death.

Tall Mountains, Cold Nights, Big Hummingbirds

High in the Andes of South America, hummingbirds are rather common, accounting for roughly twenty percent of the bird species. Some are even found occasionally at elevations exceeding 16,500 feet. How can a hummingbird survive in such a rugged habitat? The answer lies in size.

High-altitude hummingbirds are noticeably larger than their low-altitude cousins. The Giant Hummingbird, for instance, is typically found at or above tree line. Measuring almost 8-1/2 inches and weighing three-fourths of an ounce, the Giant Hummingbird is—appropriately enough—the largest hummingbird in the world.

Although smaller-bodied hummingbirds may migrate up to higher altitudes in the Andes during certain times of the year, the larger-bodied ones dominate the habitat. The advantage of a larger body is clear. Large hummingbirds do not lose heat as rapidly as smaller ones. They are also capable of storing more energy for the night, which is crucial in a place where the weather can quickly turn from pleasant to treacherous, and nighttime temperatures typically dip below freezing. Nevertheless, the Giant Hummingbird, although the length of a cardinal, is still a lightweight among birds. It must spend a large portion of its day feeding. This is the fate of all hummingbirds. In order to stay alive from one day to the next, hummingbirds must eat massive quantities of food.

Energy Conservation

Torpor, a natural state of greatly reduced metabolism, is an energy-saving adaptation. And energy is critical to hummingbirds. Each night, when they go to sleep, hummingbirds must have enough food energy to run their body processes and keep warm; otherwise, they will die in the night. That's a contrast to many other birds, which can tolerate a significant decrease in air temperature and food supply for an extended period of time. Those birds use their body's fat reserves. And they fluff their downy feathers to create a layer of insulating air that keeps them warm.

Hummingbirds do not have such options. They lack downy feathers as adults, which may seem strange for a bird prone to rapid heat loss. But the lack of down actually serves a purpose. On hot days, a small-bodied animal can overheat much more rapidly than a large-bodied animal—especially hummingbirds, with body temperatures between 104° and 109°F. The lack of down feathers in hummingbirds helps in the dissipation of the excess heat. For a bird that has such a rapid metabolism, it is a crucial adaptation.

Not only do adult hummingbirds lack downy feathers, they often lack sufficient fat reserves to see them through unusually cold spells. They do, however, have a marvelous adaptation that few warm-blooded creatures do. When they are under stress, they can enter torpor, a special state which allows them to reduce the amount of energy used to run their body functions as they rest. Torpor is used when conservation of the body's energy supplies are critically important, which occurs in three main instances: when food is restricted, when the weather is cold or when hummingbirds migrate.

First, and most simply, a hummingbird may not find enough food during the day. If it doesn't have enough energy to heat its body at night, entering torpor can help it survive until morning. A second instance where torpor is used is when the weather is cold. Because heat loss can be a concern even under normal temperatures, any decrease in temperature could potentially endanger a hummingbird. To maintain normal body temperature, hummingbirds often consume more food. But cold temperatures pose an additional problem: nectar production and insect activity slow down. So, in many cases, torpor is the only option. It helps reduce the need for the metabolically expensive body heating that can use up a hummingbird's fat reserves at night. However, if a humming-bird can store enough fat during the day to enable it to maintain normal body temperature through the night, then even during cold conditions it is not likely to enter torpor. The third way hummingbirds use torpor is before and during migration, to save energy in the form of fat reserves for the long trip.

When a hummingbird begins entering torpor, it fluffs out its body feathers, bill pointing up into the air. As the bird's metabolism slows, its body temperature decreases. Some scientists speculate that the lack of insulating downy feathers may facilitate heat loss. Eventually the bird reaches a state of greatly reduced metabolic activity.

In many species of hummingbirds, body temperature can drop by 20° to 50°F when torpid. In a few species of high altitude Andean hummingbirds, body temperature may drop to a few degrees above freezing. However far the body temperature of a hummingbird drops during torpidity, this state of minimal metabolic activity significantly conserves energy, allowing the bird to make it through the night.

Hummingbirds in a state of torpor appear to be dead. In a sense, they are very close to death. Their metabolic rate is approximately 1/50 of that of an alert hummingbird. Their heart rate is decreased from a normal resting rate of roughly 500 beats per minute to a rate of between 50 and 180 beats per minute. A torpid hummingbird may even stop breathing for a short period of time.

How long a hummingbird takes to enter torpor depends on its size. The smaller the bird, the quicker it can enter into torpor—since it can dissipate body heat much more rapidly than a larger bird. In like manner, the smaller hummingbirds also come out of torpor faster than larger ones. It can take from twenty minutes to over an hour for a hummingbird to emerge from torpor.

Calliope Hummingbird

Torpor's Tradeoffs

People once thought that all hummingbirds entered torpor at night. But this has been disproven. Under favorable living conditions, hummingbirds will not enter torpor. The reasons are simple. A torpid hummingbird is more vulnerable to predation than a sleeping one. Also, some scientists speculate that dominant territorial species might avoid torpor to prevent being displaced by rival birds in the morning.

Karen Krebbs, Assistant Curator at the Arizona–Sonora Desert Museum in Tucson, Arizona, told us that after a cold night, sometimes a hummingbird in their exhibit does not come out of torpor in the usual period of time. To reduce the risk of the bird dying during torpor, she forces it to awaken. She puts the hummingbird in a soft cloth bag and places it in an incubator to help raise its body temperature slowly. When it revives, they feed the bird so it can recover and be returned to the exhibit.

There are some interesting twists to the hummingbirds' energy puzzle. Almost all the species of hummingbirds in the United States are migratory, spending their springs and summers North of Mexico and migrating down to Mexico and Central America in the fall. Recent research has shown that they periodically enter into torpor during fall migration to conserve energy. However, before and during the spring migration, they seem to avoid entering torpor.

Several reasons have been suggested for this behavior. One has to do with feathers. Hummingbirds' molt occurs before the long return trip to the North. Since torpor would interrupt the growth rate of new feathers, the molt would take longer. This is not too desirable since it is more difficult for a hummingbird to generate lift when it is missing flight feathers. Another possibility is that any interruption in the growth process may weaken the structure of the new feathers.

Preceding page: Ruby-throated Hummingbird

Rufous Hummingbirds

A Precarious Balance

The more scientists learn about hummingbirds and their energy needs, the more they are amazed by the way these birds survive. Among birds, hummingbirds really live "on the edge," where food and energy are concerned. Yet these tiny, high-energy birds have managed to prosper in a wide variety of habitats.

Broad-tailed Hummingbirds

Hummingbirds will investigate all sorts of objects on their daily search for nectar. In aviaries, captive hummingbirds approach visitors' colorful shirts, purses, hats and hair bows. At Ramsey Canyon Preserve in Arizona, immature hummingbirds hover in front of brake lights in the parking lot. Occasionally, hummingbirds even fly into the bookstore, checking out the empty hummingbird feeders on display!

What nectar sources hummingbirds ultimately choose and why they choose them has implications not just for the birds but for flowering plants. Because, like bees, hummingbirds are pollinators; they help plants exchange pollen to reproduce. As a hummingbird laps nectar from a flower, its body brushes against one or more of the flower's anthers. Pollen is transferred from plant to bird. Later, when the bird visits another flower, this pollen may be transferred from bird back to plant. If the transferred pollen grain is from a plant of the same species, pollination occurs.

Hummingbirds and plants have a mutualistic relationship. They both gain from their interaction; birds receive nectar and the plants are pollinated.

So Many Choices

Not all nectars are created equal, and not all flowers are the exclusive domain of hummingbirds. Bees, ants, butterflies, bats, moths and beetles are also attracted to nectar-producing flowers. Yet there are distinct differences between flowers that are pollinated primarily by hummingbirds and those pollinated by other animals.

Ruby-throated Hummingbird

One noticeable difference is smell. Flowers that hummingbirds visit generally have no fragrance. Honeysuckles illustrate this trend. European honeysuckles, which are pollinated by hawkmoths, have a distinct odor. But the Pacific Northwest's wild honeysuckles, which are pollinated by hummingbirds, are odorless. The reason fragrance-free flowers evolved is simple. Although hummingbirds, according to some studies, have a sense of smell, it is probably poorly developed, as it is in most birds. It would be a waste of energy for a plant to manufacture fragrance to attract a pollinator that could barely smell it.

Besides being odorless, many hummingbird flowers are red or orange in color. Once again, honeysuckles illustrate the point. Hummingbird-pollinated honeysuckles are fiery orange, whereas hawkmoth-pollinated honeysuckles tend toward light pink and blue shades. Hummingbirds, however, will visit and feed from non-red flowers; they just visit red flowers more often, in general.

Flower selection is a learned process, particular to each individual bird. At first, young hummingbirds visit flowers of all shapes, colors and sizes. They learn through trial and error those flowers that best suit their needs. It turns out that many of the best nectar producers happen to be reddish in color. But many other hummingbird favorites, such as jewelweed, are not.

Hummingbird flowers, in general, are shaped to accommodate the birds. Trumpet-creeper exhibits the classic hummingbird flower shape: tubular. Nectaries—which produce and hold the nectar—are far back in the flower's tube. Most flying insects cannot reach the nectar deep within such flowers. But hummingbirds, with their long, narrow bill and extendible tongue, can easily access the nectaries.

Hummingbird flowers tend to hang down in loose clusters. This allows the bird plenty of maneuvering room. It also helps the hummingbirds to consume nectar more efficiently. A hummingbird visiting a upward-facing flower must extract the nectar against gravity. But in flowers that hang down, gravity can assist the hummingbird as it feeds.

The position and orientation of flowers on a plant often dictates the flight behavior of hummingbirds. When given the chance, hummingbirds will perch while feeding. Hummingbird flowers, however, usually lack perches, so hummingbirds must hover to feed.

Although color and shape may cue hummingbirds to try a particular flower, what keeps them coming back is the sugar content of the nectar. Studies show that sugar content is one of the most important factors in a hummingbird's choice of flowers. Flowers with nectar of a sugar content less than thirteen percent are usually ignored.

These characteristics of hummingbird flowers all seem to discourage, or at least not attract, other pollinators. (A plant, after all, is not well served by wasting nectar on animals other than its pollinators.) The color red is not attractive to bees, which cannot see colors in the red end of the spectrum. The deep nectaries in the flowers are hard for many insects to reach. The lack of a perch makes nectar reservoirs inaccessible to butterflies, which can see red, but need a perch to feed.

In these ways, evolution ensures that certain flowers reserve their precious nectar—and pollen—primarily for the hummingbirds that pollinate them. But no system is perfect. Lack of a suitable perch doesn't deter hummingbird moths. These moths have evolved a hovering habit, which allows them to dine from hummingbird flowers. Not only do they fool the flower's evolutionary safeguards, they often fool people, who mistake these large, hovering moths for hummingbirds.

Anna's Hummingbird

Why Red?

A common misconception is that hummingbirds only feed from red flowers and instinctively prefer the color red. Although many hummingbird-pollinated flowers are reddish in hue, hummingbirds will also visit yellow, blue, orange, violet, green, and white blossoms.

Studies have shown that hummingbirds have a preferred order of floral characteristics. Position and orientation of a plant and its flowers seem to be most important. Put simply, if a hummingbird cannot easily reach a group of flowers, it will not feed from them. Flowers that are easily available to the hummingbird are visited again and again. With their good short- and long-term spatial memories, hummingbirds can remember the location of a good flower patch. Hummingbirds returning from their winter roosting grounds have even been seen visiting the location of a favorite hummingbird feeder before it was up or a patch of perennial flowers before they had bloomed.

The next important attribute of a flower is its nectar's sugar concentration: too sweet a nectar, and the hummingbird cannot efficiently feed because the nectar is thick and slow-running; too dilute, and it is not energetically worth consuming. Color, it turns out, is third in importance—a mere cue for selection, not an overriding, innate preference.

The subsidiary role of color leads to a question: If position and sugar concentration are more important than color, why are so many hummingbird flowers red? Scientists are not sure of the exact answer, but it is likely that there are several evolutionary reasons. As already mentioned, although butterflies can see the color red, bees cannot. In plants that are primarily pollinated by hummingbirds, red flowers reduce the chance of nectar robbery by bees. Red flowers also may stand out against the green background of fields and forests, making them easier for birds to see.

And plants pollinated by hummingbirds may gain an evolutionary advantage by producing red flowers because the color red may act as a flag to hummingbirds that have learned to associate the color of a flower with its sugary reward.

Several researchers have proposed an important function for the color red: Colors at the red end of the spectrum absorb more solar energy than colors at the blue end. They speculate that the red flowers may maximize the absorption of nectar-warming solar energy. This may play a very important role where cool morning temperatures can cause the nectar in flowers to become thick and difficult on which to feed.

Whatever the reasons for the predominance of red hues in hummingbird flowers, it is clear that it does not play a unique role in attracting hummingbirds.

In North America, many of the flowers used by migratory hummingbirds are not red. It may be that over time, the use of red in floral coloration offered many evolutionary advantages to plants. Hummingbirds, through their frequent exploration of alternative food sources, learned that red flowers and sweet nectar can go hand in hand.

Calliope Hummingbird

Sweet Ambrosia

Although brightly colored flowers serve as advertisements to hummingbirds, it is the sweet nectar that makes them repeat customers. Nectar is a complex substance: much more than just sugar and water. Many nectars contain three types of sugar: sucrose, glucose, and fructose. Some nectars also contain small quantities of amino acids, fats, antioxidants and other compounds. Nectar composition varies from plant species to species. It may also vary within a species depending on the health of the plant, the condition of the soil and the amount of water a plant receives.

Hummingbird flowers typically have a sugar concentration between twenty and twenty-five percent. Interestingly enough, flowers pollinated mostly by insects are even sweeter; they have sugar concentrations around forty percent. Hummingbirds will at times feed on these flowers. But these flowers generally produce less nectar, and the hummingbirds face competition for them.

It seems strange that hummingbird flowers would have a lower sugar concentration than other flowers. But some scientists have suggested an evolutionary reason for this difference: if a plant's flowers had a higher sugar concentration, the hummingbird's energy needs would be satisfied quickly. It would not need to visit—and pollinate—as many flowers. For plants, this would be a disadvantage, because the pollen would not be widely dispersed and exchanged.

Another possible reason hummingbird nectars are lower in sugar is that it may decrease nectar robbery by bees. Hummingbird flowers with particularly long, tubular corollas are more bee-proof and tend to have higher sugar concentrations.

Controlled studies using hummingbird feeders have shown that some North American hummingbird species prefer much higher concentrated nectars than those that occur in the wild. But feeding from a feeder in the laboratory is much different from feeding from a wild flower. Viscosity may play less of a role in a feeder; more studies need to be done.

Like honey, nectar is affected by temperature. The colder the temperature, the thicker the nectar becomes. Lower sugar concentrations in wild flowers may be an adaptation that allows for hummingbirds to feed in the chilly morning air or when temperatures drop. Some hummingbird flowers track the sun. By keeping oriented toward the direct rays of the sun, a flower may increase the temperature of its nectar, thereby decreasing the nectar's viscosity.

Broad-tailed Hummingbird

Rufous Hummingbird

Of Bills and Tongues

Contrary to popular belief, hummingbirds do not suck nectar through a straw-like bill. Instead, hummingbirds use their tongues to lap nectar. The tongue of a hummingbird is about the length of the bird's bill. But a stretchy attachment called the hyoid apparatus allows the tongue to be extended about a "bill's length." This enables hummingbirds to reach nectar deep within a flower. However, hummingbirds usually only stick their tongues out a little bit to feed.

Partway down its length, a hummingbird's tongue forks, ending in two fringed feeding tips. When a hummingbird pushes its tongue into a flower nectary, the nectar flows into the grooved channels on each fork. The bill is then opened and the tongue is retracted, still carrying the nectar. The hummingbird closes its bill and extends its tongue once again. The nectar, still in the tongue, is squeezed back into the bird's mouth as the tongue is forced through the closed bill.

In North America, the bill shapes of almost all regularly occurring hummingbird species are similar. (A noticeable exception is the Lucifer Hummingbird, whose bill is noticeably decurved—meaning it curves downward.) In North America, no one hummingbird species specializes in feeding on a particular hummingbird plant, and no one native plant species is adapted for a particular hummingbird. Many different hummingbird species can feed from the various hummingbird plants in their range.

In the tropics, some hummingbirds have more exclusive relationships with flowers. High in the Ecuadorian Andes, the Sword-billed Hummingbird uses its five-inch bill to feed from an extremely long, tubular flower. The Sword-bill has the longest bill of any hummingbird, and has no competition from other hummingbird species for the nectar of this particular plant. Bill shape and flower shape can also correspond like a lock and key. The White-tipped Sickle-bill, which has an extremely decurved bill, feeds from flowers with a similarly curved shape.

Bills can vary tremendously among hummingbirds. With a bill measuring less than one-third of an inch, the Purple-backed Thornbill has the shortest bill of any hummingbird. It feeds from short flowers that are adapted for insect pollination. There is even an Avocet-bill Hummingbird, with a bill that curves up at the tip, and a Tooth-billed Hummingbird which has a serrated bill that has been compared to a drawn-out pair of needle-nosed pliers!

Some hummingbirds, such as the Purple-crowned Fairy are professional nectar robbers. They have short, sharp bills for piercing the bases of flowers. They get the nectar, but do not pollinate the plant.

Magnificent Hummingbird

From a Plant's Perspective

Hummingbird plants are adapted to avoid wasting pollen and stigma space where pollen can attach. Different plant species are structured to deposit or receive pollen from different parts of hummingbirds' bodies. One plant species may dust the hummingbird's chin, another may touch the throat, while another may dust the bill or back of the head. This strategy helps to minimize pollen waste and maximize the chances of pollen being delivered to the proper stigma.

People often think of plants as passive organisms controlled by the animals of the world. But the ways plants have evolved to use hummingbirds as pollen couriers is nothing short of remarkable. For plants, using birds as pollinators has its pros and cons. Ornithophilous flowers—those pollinated by birds—tend to have long-lived flowers that are larger and more colorful than insect-pollinated ones. Therefore, pollination by birds is costly, in terms of energy, for a plant. Nevertheless, bird pollination does have it benefits. Birds, unlike insects, can actively forage—and thereby pollinate—even in rainy, windy or cold weather. Birds have the potential to transport pollen over very long distances. Birds also have good memories and long life spans compared to insects. Year after year, a bird may remember and return to lucrative flower patches. Plants can benefit from this "repeat business" over several blooming seasons. No wonder most hummingbird plants are perennials.

Buff-bellied Hummingbird

FOUR
TERRITORIALITY AND COURTSHIP

Flitting, chirping, chattering, diving, swooping, and battling, humming-birds are among the most aggressive of all birds. Their fiery nature was admired by the Aztecs, who believed that when an Aztec warrior died in battle, he turned into a hummingbird. These warrior-birds were said to fight a daily battle against the darkness to ensure the sun would again light the world, and bring the day. As a reward for their efforts, the hummingbirds' feathers are illuminated by the sun with the bright, jeweled colors they wear.

Turf Wars: Hummingbird Territories

Whether hummingbirds battle the darkness or not, they will certainly challenge animal foes. First and foremost, they chase off other hummingbirds. But bees, butterflies, wasps, orioles, crows, kingbirds, even Sharp-shinned Hawks are fair game. People, cats and lizards have also reportedly been dive-bombed by hummingbirds.

Hummingbirds are quick to defend their territories, which may encompass a garden, a field of flowers, a flowering bush or tree, a particularly nectar-rich clump of flowers or their nest. Rufous Hummingbirds have been known to defend trees with trunks filled with sapsucker holes.

Both males and females may establish territories, although males are by far the most demonstrative in territorial defense. In many species, males and females set up territories in adjacent, although slightly different habitats, so they are not in constant, direct competition. Black-chinned females, for instance, nest in canyon-bottom woodlands, whereas males set up territories in more open, sloped spots. Males may defend large territories throughout the breeding season. Females defend their feeding territories early in the nesting season. However, once they get busy with the chores of taking care of nest and nestlings, females' territoriality seems to taper off. They don't always bother to defend feeding spots, although they chase predators and other hummingbirds away from the area near the nest.

Not all hummingbirds establish territories. After all, defending a territory must be worth it, energetically. Many hummingbird species are pushed out of favorable spots by more aggressive, territorial birds. So these birds must gather nectar from a large, scattered area. Instead of trying to defend such a wide area, they spend their foraging time flying from place to place, gathering nectar. They follow an established daily route, or "trapline," gathering food from certain widely dispersed trees or flowers.

Among hummingbird species, some tend to be territorial and others tend to be trapliners. But most species can adopt either foraging strategy, according to the food available and how stiff the competition is with other birds. Also, differences may exist between the sexes; in a Colorado study, Broad-tailed males set up territories, whereas females tended to trapline.

There is an interesting side note: scientists measuring wing dimensions of traplining species and territorial hummingbirds have discovered a correlation. Wings of trapliners are better suited, in terms of design, for the long flight from flower clump to flower clump. The wings of territorial hummingbird species have dimensions better fit for the hovering, chasing, diving, and maneuvering required for defending a territory.

A territory itself can vary season to season, day to day, and even hour to hour. Migratory hummingbirds set up territories on their summer breeding grounds but may not do so at their winter residences. At stopovers on their migration routes, migrating hummingbirds often set up temporary feeding territories that last only a few days. In numerous experiments, hummingbirds have been shown to adjust the geographical size of their territories as nectar sources fluctuate. By covering up some flowers with plastic bags, scientists eliminated

Black-chinned Hummingbird

nectar sources from hummingbirds' territories. The hummingbirds promptly expanded their territories to encompass more nectar-producing flowers. Once the flowers were uncovered and the nectar was available again, the territories shrunk. These studies clearly showed that hummingbirds will adjust the size of their territory according to the food available day to day. Male hummingbirds with territories also have been known to leave their territories for short periods in the morning and evening to forage more widely for food.

Costa's Hummingbird

Vocalizations

Songbirds such as sparrows and cardinals declare their territories by singing their claim from a perch high on a bush or tree. Some hummingbirds do the same. But many of the vocal sounds North American hummingbirds make are hardly melodic enough to qualify as songs at all. Chirps, ticks, cheeps, buzzes and clacks are the norm. An Anna's voice is squeaky; the Costa's is a

bit of a whistle. Hummingbirds' voices have been likened to the sound of a file on metal, a nail scratching a tin can, and other less than favorable comparisons. Much of the sounds hummingbirds make are not vocal, but instead are produced by their feathers as they fly or dive. Their wings produce the humming. The sound of a Broad-tailed Hummingbird in flight is often compared to the noise of a bullet whistling past.

Flight Displays

In addition to vocalizations, hummingbirds flash their bright feathers and carry out flight displays. Hummingbirds often spread their tail feathers and gorget—the iridescent feathers around their chin—to maximize their visual impact. Because feathers that appear dark in the shade appear brightly colored in the proper light, displaying hummingbirds often orient themselves toward the sun when perching, singing, hovering or diving. On cloudy, overcast days, Anna's Hummingbirds may turn in any direction to dive. But on clear days, they face the direction of the sun.

Hummingbirds carry out two main types of flight displays: shuttle flights and dives. During both these displays, the wings are vibrated so that feathers make various buzzing, popping, and trilling noises. The shuttle flight, which is often used in courtship, consists of hovering horizontally back and forth in front of or above the female. Dives, for which male Anna's Hummingbirds are best known, are even more spectacular events. An Anna's will fly upward seventy-five feet or more in the air, sing a little, hover at the apex, then dive. His wings make a dramatic, metallic popping noise as he dives. Then he pulls up in an arc, just short of the target female or intruder.

Rufous Hummingbirds

Aggressive Behavior

If vocalizations, dives, and chases don't get the job done, hummingbirds are not above using a little "muscle" to kick other hummingbirds out of the territory. Battles often start in midair, where the birds pummel, push and scratch one another with their claws. Bills can also be weapons.

Hummingbirds locked in combat may flutter and tumble to the ground and scuffle in the dirt. Or they may rise back up for yet another midair round. Despite the fierce look of these fights, the birds rarely seem harmed, other than a few lost feathers. But there have been no consistent follow-up studies on the birds, so no one really knows.

Fierce defense of a territory seems to be a central part of male hummingbirds' lives. Among young males, territorial scuffles start early in life. Nestlings only a few days out of the nest begin carrying out displays, battles and aggressive behavior; but they certainly are not the refined rituals of older males. Establishing and defending a territory provides a male hummingbird with food. But the quality of the male's territory also likely plays a role in attracting females for mating. The males that establish territories attract the females, whereas the "drifters," which do not establish territories, are not likely to find mates.

Courtship And Mating

Courtship is among the least known and understood of hummingbird behaviors. Indeed, some scientists would say that some hummingbird species' behavior barely qualifies as courtship at all. Males and females spend almost all their time apart, only meeting for a brief interlude during mating season. The birds rarely touch. Their interaction appears as much aggressive as sexual. What complicates the study of courtship is that it's sometimes unclear whether a male hummingbird is diving and displaying to drive off other males or to impress a nearby female. As of yet, the courtship behaviors of most North American hummingbird species have not been studied. So the dynamics of their relationships are poorly understood.

So far, naturalists can only guess that the behavior of many North American hummingbirds parallels that of the well-studied Anna's species. Male and female Anna's Hummingbirds establish separate territories. The female begins building the nest in hers. Then, when she's ready, she approaches the male's territory. The male may respond in a variety of ways, even chasing her off like a rival male, at first. Often, he will carry out

Magnificent Hummingbird

dramatic aerial displays, such as diving or shuttle displays. Climbing, power diving, showing his colorful feathers in the best possible light, the male courts the female. Eventually, the female "allows" him to chase her toward her territory. There, or nearby, copulation occurs while the female is perched. It is a brief event, easily missed by an observer. The male mounts the female's back for just a few seconds.

Once copulation is over, the female returns to nest building. She will lay the eggs, and raise and feed the young all on her own. The male flies back to his territory, where he may mate with several more females as the season progresses. Broad-tailed Hummingbirds have been observed courting at least six different females in a season.

A few hummingbirds have more elaborate courtship rituals. As many as twenty-five male Long-tailed Hermits—a hummingbird common in tropical forests—may gather in a small areas, each on its own perch. The birds sing almost all day long, competing for the attention of a female. This shared mating area is called a lek. Once the females have selected a male, mating occurs. Lek behavior has also been observed among Anna's, Blue-throated, White-eared, Berylline and Violet-crowned hummingbirds, whose ranges extend into southeastern Arizona.

Territoriality among a few species, such as Rufous, Anna's and Broad-tailed Hummingbirds, has been well studied. But overall, like courtship, the territorial behavior of most hummingbirds is not well understood. It is indeed strange that such well-loved birds live such hidden, little-known lives.

Anna's Hummingbird

FIVE
NESTING AND RAISING YOUNG

To find a hummingbird nest you have to be sharp-eyed. A fellow birder pointed out the first hummingbird nest we ever saw. It was twenty feet off the ground, near a wetland boardwalk at Huntley Meadows Park in Virginia. Even with direction, however, the nest was difficult to find. We squinted at it for several minutes before we recognized its shape. The mother bird, which was sitting on the nest, was only visible by her tail tip and beak tip, which jutted out beyond the nest edge.

Not all hummingbird nests are hidden from view. In the Caribbean, where many people keep windows and doors open to get the ocean breeze, hummingbirds sometimes nest indoors. They've nested and raised young inside houses, offices, and schools, in vases, light fixtures, even chandeliers! There are even some reports in North America of hummingbirds nesting in barns, outdoor dance halls and porch light fixtures.

You're more likely to find a nest in a tree, bush, or cactus. If you do see one, locate a comfortable vantage point, at a respectful distance from the nest. If you notice that the mother hummingbird is not returning to the nest to feed the young, you are probably too close. Chipping and squeaking noises from the mother, or even dive bombing, pulling out of the dive a few inches above your head, will also alert you to this fact.

Hummingbird Home Life

Hummingbirds grow up in single-parent families. Once the male has mated with the female, he returns to his territory. That's the only part in family life he plays. Although isolated reports of male Rufous and Ruby-throated Hummingbirds helping defend nests and incubate eggs have been reported. One person witnessed a male Anna's feeding young. But these reports are the exception. All in all, it's the hummingbird mother who is the nest builder, egg layer and nurturer of the family.

Broad-tailed Hummingbird

Research has shown that the breeding season of hummingbirds is strongly correlated with the availability of food. Because the energetic costs of nest building, egg laying and raising young is high, it is advantageous to time such activities when food resources are abundant. A mother hummingbird must be able to find nectar and insects for herself and her chicks quickly, so she can rush back to the nest to care for them. For this reason, the timing of nesting varies among species and habitats. For instance, Anna's Hummingbirds are year-round residents throughout most of their North American range. They are North America's earliest nesters, even before owls. In the southern part of their range, they begin nesting as early as December or January. However, in the northern part of their range, Anna's Hummingbirds may not nest until months later. The availability of reliable food resources is the limiting factor.

Nest Building

If you visit the Hummingbird House at the Arizona–Sonora Desert Museum in early spring, you might be in for a surprise. Hummingbirds occasionally swoop down on visitors to pick up stray hairs or loose sweater threads which are then incorporated into their nests. Sweater yarn, string, cotton, paper towel strips, clothes dryer lint, and even poodle fur—collected from dog groomers, not plucked from unsuspecting dogs—also are favorite nesting materials for a few captive hummingbirds.

The nests built by wild North American hummingbirds are generally cup-shaped and less than two inches wide, and are often compared in dimensions to a golf ball cut in half. Construction materials include leaves, grass, pine needles, roots, animal fur, moss, insect cocoons and plant down—the fluffy cottony material of milkweeds and other plants. Hummingbirds sometimes recycle their old nests, even building on top of old ones. Such behavior can significantly reduce the amount of energy required in gathering nesting material. Hummingbirds have even been reported stealing nesting material from other birds.

Nest construction varies. Some nests are made almost entirely of soft materials such as animal hair. Others are formed of rough materials, but lined with soft moss, feathers or plant down. The outside of a nest is usually camouflaged with small bits of lichen, moss or bark.

One more component is essential for hummingbird nests, as Assistant Curator Karen Krebbs found out long ago. She had just moved the hummingbirds into a new exhibit space. Nesting season was just beginning and so the early nesters began building nests. But the nests they built were poorly

constructed. Some were literally falling apart, endangering the eggs. She had to prop a few nests up with wire, to prevent a total loss.

Understandably concerned, Krebbs and her boss, Peter Siminski, tried to figure out what was wrong. The nests in the old exhibit had been fine. After some puzzling, they took a guess at the missing element: spider webs. The building was so new, spiders had not moved in yet.

To quickly correct the problem, Krebbs and her assistants collected spider webs and put them in the hummingbird room. The nests improved. But still, they weren't quite perfect. Krebbs, with the help of a specialist, collected appropriate spiders, and introduced them to the room. Once fresh spider webs were on hand, the hummingbirds made more compact, solid nests, glued with the sticky silk. With the problem solved, most of the eggs and young were safely raised.

Sticky spider webs are the "glue" that holds hummingbird nests together. The fiber is also used by hummingbirds to bind their nests to tree branches, leaves, rocks or cacti. A few tropical species have even stranger habits; they wrap their nests around palm leaves, or suspend them by threads from trees, or build them inside hard-to-reach caves.

Each species has its own general preferences, suited to its habitat. In one canyon for instance, Violet-crowned Hummingbirds nested exclusively toward the edges of Arizona sycamores. Black-chinned Hummingbirds also preferred Arizona sycamores but utilized the inside parts as well as the edges of the trees. Costa's Hummingbirds chose to nest in small trees located in drier parts of the canyon.

How far above the ground the nests of North American hummingbirds are located ranges from a few inches to seventy feet, depending on the species and habitat. Broad-billed Hummingbirds nest only about three-and-a-half feet off the ground, whereas Violet-crowned Hummingbirds nest an average of twenty feet above the ground.

Hummingbirds usually build their nests a respectable distance from each other. Sometimes, however, hummingbirds will nest closer than expected. As many as twenty Rufous Hummingbird nests reportedly have been clustered together, within a few yards of each other.

Some nesting hummingbirds must endure quite cold temperatures: Calliope and Broad-tailed Hummingbirds because they nest in high-elevation woodlands; Anna's Hummingbirds because they nest early in the year. Nests of these birds are almost always positioned underneath a relatively thick branch or other type of overhang, probably in order to reduce loss of heat to the chilly, clear nighttime sky. Overhangs may play an even more important role during the day, shading eggs from too much sun which could overheat them.

Rufous Hummingbird

The most important factor, however, in maintaining a warm nest during cold nights is the nest material itself. The nest, with an incubating female in place, provides sufficient insulation to keep the eggs warm at night. Some species increase the thickness of the nests to accommodate colder environments.

Watching a nest being built is a rare treat. The female carries nesting materials in her bill to the site. She pokes, prods and twists tidbits into place. She wraps the nest with sticky spider silk. She stamps her feet to press down material within the nest. As she works, she moves her body back and forth within the nest, to develop the cup-shaped crevice for the eggs. Many hummingbirds will also build new nests on old nests, or renovate old nests for use. These nests may be their own from a previous season or those of other hummingbirds.

From start to finish, nest building can take anywhere from one day to over two weeks, depending on the species and the individual bird. Usually, though, about one week is required. Some birds construct their nest in long sessions, while others will work in short bouts over many days. Even after laying her eggs, a female hummingbird will continue adding material to the nest. Responsible parents, after all, keep their homes in good repair.

From Egg to Chick

Once the female has mated, it takes a day or two for an egg to develop. Hummingbirds generally lay two eggs: first one egg, then a day or so later, the second. There are a few records of Black-chinned Hummingbirds laying from one to three eggs but two is the most common. Hummingbird eggs are tiny, averaging less than half an inch in length and less than a quarter-ounce in weight—about the size of a jelly bean. Despite their small size, the eggs are a considerable burden for these tiny birds. Two hummingbird eggs can weigh fourteen or more percent of the mother's body weight!

Hummingbird eggs are slightly pink and translucent at first, and turn whiter as they mature. Like most other birds, female hummingbirds incubate their eggs. Most hummingbirds begin incubation after the first egg is laid. The eggs will hatch in the same order as they were laid and roughly twenty-four to forty-eight hours apart. Sometimes, however, hummingbirds will not start incubating the eggs until the second egg is laid. That way, the two eggs will hatch at about the same time.

Generally, an egg temperature of about 90°F is maintained. On cold days, she warms them. On hot, sunny days, overheating may be the problem instead; so the mother stands just close enough to shade the eggs and keep them cool. Using her feet or bill, the mother turns the eggs each day, to even out the temperature, and to prevent the embryos from sticking to the shell.

But the mother can't incubate the eggs all the time. She needs food to survive. Hummingbird bodies burn up a lot of energy, even at rest. During the daytime, an incubating hummingbird spends twenty to forty percent of her time away from the nest, but only leaves the nest unattended for five minutes or so at a time.

In hummingbirds that nest where the evening temperatures are very cold, an interesting phenomenon occurs: Incubating females rarely enter torpor at night to survive the cold as other hummingbirds do. The incubating female must keep her body temperature high to keep the eggs warm. To avoid going into torpor, she must spend the latter part of the day consuming extra nectar to give her energy for the night. This, plus the nest insulation, helps keep her and her eggs warm. Some studies have shown that even if the mother does go into torpor, she controls her drop in body temperature, maintaining the temperature of the eggs at around 44°F. The developing embryos are usually not harmed as long as this does not happen very often.

Black-chinned Hummingbird eggs

Baby Hummingbirds

After about two weeks, the incubation period is over and the eggs hatch. An egg tooth, a special tip on the bird's bill, helps it tap its way through the shell. The mother bird may carry the shell pieces out of the nest and deposit them far away. In this way, she reduces the probability that predators will locate the nest.

Baby hummingbirds don't look much like their colorful, graceful, parents. They hatch blind and naked, and are totally dependent on their mother. In the first few days after hatching, a chick still has a visible yolk sac. It disappears as the food in it is used up, and the sac is absorbed into the chick's body.

According to Krebbs, baby hummingbirds resemble "brown raisins with huge heads and eyes." The chicks must be kept warm by their mother. So when she is not out gathering food, she broods (sits on them). She also uses her body to shield them from rain and hot sun.

Unlike most other baby birds, hummingbirds never grow very many fluffy, downy feathers to help keep them warm. They have just a few scraggly ones at birth. It's a week or two before enough adult feathers grow in and their bodies start producing sufficient heat to keep them warm on their own. At this stage the mother usually stops brooding her young. Besides, the nest is now too crowded to fit the entire family.

As a single mother, the female must leave the babies unattended at times to go out and catch insects and gather nectar for food. For the first couple days after the birds hatch, the mother almost exclusively feeds tiny insects to her young. She begins to add more and more nectar to her chicks' diet as they grow. One reason for this preference toward insect meals may be that the rapidly growing chicks need sufficient protein and fat to develop properly.

An interesting behavior has been documented in Anna's Hummingbirds. When the chicks are several days old, the mother Anna's will feed her chicks nectar primarily in the morning and early afternoon. But as the day goes on, she will switch to feeding them primarily small insects.

Depending on the developmental stage of the chicks, the mother's feeding behavior of her young differs. For about the first five days, the chicks are inactive in the nest. When the mother returns with food, she must stimulate them in order to get them to gape, or open their mouths wide. She does this by using her bill to touch the nestlings behind their eye-bulges. Immediately they open their mouths and she feeds them. Inserting her bill

Ruby-throated Hummingbird

into a chick's mouth, she regurgitates food she's gathered. The food goes down the chick's throat and into its crop, a food storage pouch on its neck. Once full, the crop distends, making an alarming-looking lump on the side of the tiny chick's neck. But the crop serves a useful function, allowing the baby bird to process food at its own pace.

Around the sixth day, her feeding changes. The chicks' adult feathers have started to grow. Although they will still be blind for a couple more days, they now sense when their mother arrives by the air motion from her wings which stimulates them to gape.

As the chicks grow bigger, the soft, flexible nest stretches to accommodate their bulk. By the time the chicks are ready to fledge, fly away from the nest, they are practically falling out of the nest. They sit on the edge of the nest and stretch and flap their wings. Three to four weeks after hatching, the immature birds take flight, never to return to their nest again. Even at the start, they're not bad fliers. But their landings certainly lack grace. You can recognize a baby hummingbird by its awkward behavior, its short bill and short tail.

Unlike most nestlings, young hummingbirds never peep or make begging calls to their mother while in the nest. One scientist speculates that lack of vocalization may be an adaptation to reduce the chance of being discovered by predators. Hummingbird nests and their young are relatively exposed. Supporting this line of reasoning is the observation that in the few tropical species of hummingbirds that build enclosed, domed nests, the young chicks give begging calls very shortly after hatching.

Once the young have fledged, their mother will continue feeding them for two to three more weeks before they are entirely on their own. You might hear peeping noises from shrubs or trees as these "teenagers" now beg food from their parent. In rare instances, adult hummingbirds other than mothers have been seen feeding young hummingbirds as well.

The mother does not teach young hummingbirds feeding skills in any ritualized way. But the young hummingbirds certainly seem to observe the behavior of their mother and other adults closely. They may, in some cases, follow the adults' examples. But much of what they do is partly by instinct, and partly through trial, error and experience.

Hazards of Survival

Despite all the adaptations hummingbirds have evolved to enable them to survive, their reproductive success is low. There are many things that can go wrong during nesting. Severe storms, unusual cold spells and low food supplies are a few factors that lead to failure. But out of all nest failures, nearly eighty percent are attributable to predation.

An egg or a baby hummingbird is a bite-sized morsel for birds, mice, snakes, squirrels, cats, lizards, and even large ants that have been known to eat or carry off young hummingbirds. A few reports indicate that spiders may occasionally, though rarely, kill nestlings too, although it is not clear whether they are then eaten.

In the United States, only about forty percent of hummingbird eggs hatch and grow into chicks that survive to fledge. Some species have a higher

Ruby-throated Hummingbird

success rate, and others lower. Out of those nests that are successful, it is not unusual for only one young to live to fledge.

If a hummingbird loses her first set of chicks, she may breed again and lay eggs in the same nest. Or, she may build another nest to start her family. Several North American hummingbird species—including Black-chinned Hummingbirds, Ruby-throated Hummingbirds, White-eared Hummingbirds, Blue-throated Hummingbirds and Broad-tailed Hummingbirds—have been seen caring for two nests at once. Usually, one nest is full of nestlings close to fledging while the others are still eggs.

Eggs are by far more vulnerable than nestlings. Once a nestling has fledged, its chances of survival are even greater. In fact, in North America, there are no predators known to specialize in eating hummingbirds. Hummingbirds are highly maneuverable fliers and quick enough to elude most predators. But, once in a while, fledged hummingbirds will get caught. There are accounts of hummingbirds being killed and eaten by predators including cats, frogs, hawks, brown-crested flycatchers, road-runners and even praying mantises. Although these animals are certainly natural predators, their success at catching hummingbirds is very low.

No one knows exactly how long hummingbirds live. Experts guess that in the wild they may survive four or five years on average. However, Arizona bird banders have caught the same birds year after year. One Broad-tailed Hummingbird was recaptured twelve years after the time it was first banded; but this long a life span is probably uncommon. In captivity, hummingbirds have been known to live ten to twelve years. That's a considerably long life span for small animals with such high metabolism.

Anna's Hummingbirds

Calliope Hummingbird

In Indiana, children plant hummingbird flowers outside their school. In Arizona, a retired couple hangs a feeder outside their motor home. In California, a naturalist refills a bank of feeders, while hundreds of hummingbirds hover and wait. All over the United States and Canada, people are putting up feeders for hummingbirds, and gardeners are planting flowers with the nectar needs of hummingbirds in mind. Hummingbird feeders and plantings are available in catalogs, feed stores and even local drug and grocery stores. The bird feeders and gardens not only help the birds, but also give people the joy of close encounters with these marvelous birds.

Feeder Basics

The equipment for hummingbird feeding is not expensive. But it does need to be properly maintained. If feeders are not cleaned regularly, mold and bacteria can build up in them and harm the hummingbirds. It takes time and effort to feed hummingbirds properly. Putting up feeders requires a commitment, much like the care of a pet.

Anna's Hummingbirds

Some people feed hummingbirds on a major scale. The Patons, a couple living near the Patagonia–Sonoita Creek Preserve, maintain six large-capacity feeders for hummingbirds. Hundreds of hummingbirds accept their invitation every day. Fortunately, the Patons, at the time of this writing, also have a standing invitation to bird watchers as well. By the bus and carload, hummingbird enthusiasts arrive at their yard, walk around their house, and settle into chairs to watch the show. The last time we were there, the yard was packed with hummingbirds—and hummingbirders. Dozens of birds whizzed past our ears and probably hundreds more perched in nearby trees. Seeing so many birds was dazzling, awe-inspiring, and a little bit like standing in the midst of a noisy swarm of bees. Of course, you need not undertake feeding hummingbirds on such a big scale. Although we should warn you, this pleasant hobby can be addictive!

The basics of hummingbird feeding are really quite simple. Several different feeder designs are available, ranging from hanging bottles with red flowers on the spouts, to plastic feeders that look like thick disks with slots in the side, to egg-shaped, high-volume feeders. Any of these feeders will work. Just be sure the ones you purchase are easy to take apart and clean. The fewer crevices and cracks where mold can develop, the better. Red parts help attract the birds (although hummingbirds will come to feeders without them, once they've discovered they contain nectar). To increase your chances of success, just remember these simple points:

- To make nectar, mix four parts water to one part white sugar. (This closely approximates the sugar content of natural flower nectar.) Boil one to two minutes and let cool. (If you boil longer, you'll need to add extra water to make up for the water lost as steam.)

- Do not use honey in feeders. Honey can harbor fungi that cause hummingbirds' tongues to swell. This may kill the birds. Also, do not use artificial sweeteners, because they offer no caloric benefit to hummingbirds.

- Do not use red dye in the feeder solution. Many hummingbird experts are concerned about its use and strongly recommend you avoid it. The red parts of commercial feeders should be sufficient to attract the birds.

- Clean hummingbird feeders at least once a week—twice in hot weather. To clean, use bottle brushes or pipe cleaners and a solution of ten parts water to one part bleach. Be sure to rinse thoroughly with water after cleaning with bleach.

- Hang feeders in the shade, away from wind.

- Place feeders three to seven feet off the ground, where you can reach them. Feeders may hang from a tree, a post, a clothesline, or any convenient place.

Hummingbirds need more than sugar and water to survive. However, you need not worry about your sugar water feeders spoiling hummingbirds' diets. They gain the rest of the nutrients they need from eating insects and spiders between their nectar meals.

If you have seen hummingbirds in your yard already, put the feeder near where you've seen them. Or, place the feeder close to a clump of red, orange or yellow flowers. Although the red plastic parts on commercial feeders are usually enough to attract inquisitive hummingbirds, some people paint extra red decorations on their feeder bulb, or even hang red plastic streamers from the feeder. But if hummingbirds are in the area, you may attract them without any such help.

Don't be disappointed if you do not attract hummingbirds your first summer. Attracting hummingbirds in the eastern United States and Midwest can be a hit-or-miss affair. Sometimes hummingbird plantings can be more successful. Ruby-throated Hummingbirds might buzz in now and then to visit bee balm and jewelweed. In many parts of the country, hummingbird density is higher and they quickly find feeders.

If an individual hummingbird is dominating your hummingbird feeders and keeping other hummingbirds away, you might try some techniques suggested by Karen Krebbs. Put up several feeders. Hang them at different heights. Break up the space in which the birds feed. In a garden, trees, shrubs, lattices, fountains, and other physical barriers between feeders might help prevent one bird from dominating them all and excluding other birds. Alternate food sources such as hummingbird bushes and flowers help as well.

If you have trouble attracting hummingbirds to your feeders, just remember that hummingbirds are not pets and don't come on call. They may be too busy feeding on flowers in the area, or breeding and raising young elsewhere. Or, your area may not have enough flowers to attract a hummingbird that would see your feeder. Try moving your feeder around to different areas. Keep the nectar solution fresh and change it often. Then increase your chances of attracting hummingbirds by planting more flowers in your yard. Even if you don't attract hummingbirds, you will probably lure some butterflies, and have a lovely garden, too!

When to Feed

When you put up your feeders depends on whether hummingbirds are year-round residents in your area or whether they winter elsewhere. Part of the population of Anna's Hummingbirds stays in California year-round. Southeastern Arizona and parts of the southeastern United States also have a few hummingbirds during the winter. Elsewhere in North America, hummingbirds only stay during spring, summer, and early fall.

In spring, you should put up your feeders a few days or weeks before the birds typically arrive. That way, any "early birds" will have the benefit of your feeders when flowers are scarce. To get a general idea when each hummingbird species

Anna's Hummingbird

migrates, check the species profiles in this book. For more specific information on when birds arrive, contact your local Audubon chapter. Audubon societies usually keep records of such information.

When to take your feeders down depends on when birds depart from your area. Many people mistakenly believe that if they leave their feeders up too long, birds will not migrate. This concern is unfounded. Birds have an innate urge to migrate which is triggered by factors such as day length. Leaving your feeders up as long as possible, even a few weeks after the summer resident hummingbirds have left, is probably a good idea. Male hummingbirds generally migrate first, followed by females and immatures. Even if your regular summer "resident" birds have left, migrating birds and stragglers may be able to fuel-up at your feeders, helping them on their trip.

Almost every year, a few isolated cases are reported of hummingbirds spending the winter out of their normal winter range. A Ruby-throated Hummingbird spent the winter in Canada recently. A Rufous Hummingbird spent the winter in Washington, D.C. Studies of banded birds have led some naturalists to believe that most birds that stay the winter are birds that have already migrated at least part of the way. They may be off course. A wrong-way journey can leave them too exhausted to finish their trip. Whether the birds are too old, too injured, too young, too confused, or too exhausted to complete the trip, a few birds spend winters on their usual summering grounds.

Many of these birds die. Some are nursed through the winter by people faithfully replacing feeders that freeze, or rigging up heat-lamps to keep the feeder warm. Hummingbirds can survive quite cold temperatures because of their ability to go into torpor. Even in a snowstorm, hummingbirds have been known to come to feeders to feed. However, there's no question that cold weather can be deadly, wherever it occurs. For this reason, some overwintering hummingbirds are captured by people with special government permits to do so, and then kept in captivity or flown by plane to their natural habitat.

Solving Feeder Problems

For most people, the biggest problem with their hummingbird feeders is insects, and maybe an overly dominant bird. But in Portal, Arizona, the biggest problem is bears. Black bears smell the sweet liquid and maraud the feeders at night; many people have had their feeders destroyed. As a result, most residents now take down their feeders at night. Bringing feeders inside at night is also necessary in some other parts of the country where opossums and raccoons can cause problems.

Ants, bees and wasps are a more common challenge. Having a few insects in and on a hummingbird feeder is not, in itself, a problem. Hummingbirds will often bypass them to get to the food. Sometimes, however, ants, bees, yellow jackets and even butterflies become so numerous that they discourage hummingbirds from feeding.

If you do have an insect problem, first and foremost, *do not* use any insecticides or sprays on feeders. You do not want to risk poisoning the birds. Hummingbird feeding "veterans" offer the following suggestions for handling insect problems:

- Keep feeders clean. Once or twice a day, wipe off the sticky syrup the birds drip onto the feeders.

- Occasionally, even bee guards are not enough if the fluid drips on the cage. Some people add an extra wire mesh to extend the bee guard slightly and make it even harder for bees to get to the nozzle.

- Using a cotton swab, apply petroleum jelly or salad oil on the surfaces around the openings. Try not to get any in the openings where it could rub off on the bird. Also apply petroleum jelly to the string, wire or rope on which the feeder hangs. The coating makes the surface slippery and difficult for bees and wasps to hang on. (Note: Be conservative in your use of petroleum jelly. It can cause problems for hummingbirds if they get it on their bodies.)

- Ants will not usually cross water. A water "moat" around the base of a feeder pole or at the top of a feeder where the rope attaches will help keep ants away. Some feeders incorporate an ant guard for this purpose.

- To keep butterflies away from hummingbird feeders, plant butterfly plants or hang up butterfly feeders. This may draw them away from the birds' feeders. Butterfly feeders are now available in most bird catalogs.

- Use a disk-shaped hummingbird feeder. Fill it only part way with sugar water, so that the fluid level is far below the feeding holes. Bees and wasps will not be able to reach the solution, but the hummingbirds should have no problem.

You may have to try several of these suggestions to find the solution that works for your feeder and habitat.

Another common problem is domineering hummingbirds. Some species of hummingbirds tend to chase other hummingbirds away from feeders. Defending a food source is a natural behavior for territorial hummingbirds. But when one aggressive Rufous Hummingbird monopolizes several feeders, for instance, it can be frustrating to other hummingbirds and hummingbird watchers alike.

Many people put up several feeders, each at different heights. They may place one far away from the others so one bird cannot watch and defend all the feeders at once. Trial and error is necessary to work out the problem for your particular habitat and particular birds. Individual hummingbirds have recognizable, individual habits, and what solves the problem with one may not work with another.

Other visitors to hummingbird feeders are orioles. Most birders are as happy to see these dramatic orange birds as they are the hummingbirds. However, orioles can drink a substantial amount of nectar. So you may want to add an oriole feeder to your yard. Not only are oriole feeders large-capacity, they can also be filled with nectar more dilute than what you feed to hummingbirds. For orioles, one-third cup sugar to two cups water should do. Boil the solution and cool it, as you would for a hummingbird feeder. Oriole enthusiasts also hang up slices of oranges to attract these fruit-loving birds.

Hummingbird feeders have other side-benefits. We have seen Gila Woodpeckers on hummingbird feeders. Other bird watchers have had warblers, finches, cardinals, and even lizards visit their hummingbird feeders! At an inn adjacent to the Nature Conservancy's Ramsey Canyon Preserve, feeders are left up for an evening performance: nectar-feeding bats. The bats swoop in to feed, providing as much entertainment as the hummingbirds provide during the day.

Creating A Hummingbird "Hot Spot"

Hummingbird gardens bring joy to families everywhere. Good gardens can bring in forty or more hummingbirds at a time. The addition of feeders can attract even more. Planting with hummingbirds in mind may take a little more effort than just putting up feeders, but in the long run, hummingbird flowers take less maintenance than feeders and add beauty to a porch, patio or yard.

To turn your garden in to a hummingbird haven, take a look at it from a hummingbird's point of view. To a hummingbird, nectar-filled flowers are the

Preceding page: Allen's Hummingbird

Rufous Hummingbird

biggest attraction. The sound of dripping or running water attracts birds of many kinds, so a garden sprinkler may be a good bathing place. Nice high perches where hummingbirds can keep an eye on things are also favorable; poles, trees, even clotheslines will do.

Red, trumpet-shaped blossoms are the classic hummingbird flowers, and among the hummingbird's favorites. But you're not committed to an all-red garden just because you're planting for hummingbirds. Fuchsias flower in deep purple. Jewelweeds come in yellow and orange. The yellow of tree tobacco, blue of morning glories and penstemons, the pink of coral bells and columbines and the white of Solomon's seal all can lure hummingbirds and add color and variety to your garden.

Flowering trees can also be part of your plan. Many have flowers that attract hummingbirds. Strangely enough, citrus blossoms, which are neither red nor trumpet-shaped attract hummingbirds, as citrus growers have discovered. When they're in bloom, these groves are a good place to see wild hummingbirds. As many as five hummingbird species have been spotted in one grove.

Gardeners planning for the long term can landscape with trees that attract sapsuckers. Sapsuckers will take sap from apple trees, willows, paper birch, hickory and other trees. The sap wells created by the sapsuckers often attract hummingbirds. By doing this, you can enjoy the woodpeckers and the hummingbirds, and have a nice shady spot as well.

To start your hummingbird garden, visit a nursery or garden store and purchase a hummingbird wildflower mix or plant starts. Before you buy some, however, background research may be well worthwhile. Start by visiting gardens in your area and talking to people who are already gardening for hummingbirds. Speak with the curator of the local botanical garden or nature center. Contact your local Audubon Society to find out who has hummingbird gardens in your area. These people can give you a wealth of information about which plants seem to be most effective in your area for attracting hummingbirds.

Native plantings are best. They are among the most likely to thrive in the climate and soil types in your area. Another reason for using native plants is that if they escape from your garden, there's no harm done. Plants can spread from your garden through reaching roots and seeds scattered by wind, water or animals. Exotic, non-native "escapees" can wreak havoc on natural landscapes, displacing native plants that native animals need for food and shelter.

A mixture of herbs, shrubs, cascading vines and trees can give your garden a pleasing variety of shapes and colors. Just remember, you can start small, with a clump of bee balm, jewelweed or trumpet creeper vine.

Apartment-dwellers can put up window boxes of herbs such as sage, pineapple sage, monarda, and flowers such as nasturtiums. On a small patio or porch, a pot with a trellis of trumpet creeper may work. Pots or hanging baskets of fuchsia, impatiens, phlox, columbine and nicotiana are among the many possibilities. You are only limited by your imagination and what you can find at a store or through a catalog. Also, you may be able to get free plants: ask friends to share cuttings or divided plants from their hummingbird gardens!

Broad-billed Hummingbird

Anna's Hummingbird

Hummingbirds are such colorful birds, you might think they would be easy to identify. Not true. For one thing, these whirring blurs of color can whiz by quickly, making it difficult to see field marks. Females and immatures are duller in color and can be tricky to identify. Molting birds—those which are losing and replacing feathers—complicate the issue even further. And, as Sheri Williamson of Ramsey Canyon Preserve pointed out, "Sometimes hummingbirds are so covered with yellow pollen, their colors can fool you!"

Other puzzles are caused by the interbreeding of hummingbirds, which occurs more frequently than in other bird families. Hybrids—a mixture of two species—is the result of interbreeding. An even stranger sight at a hummingbird feeder is an albino hummingbird. These birds have white feathers and pink eyes. Albino Black-chinned, Allen's and Ruby-throated hummingbirds have been seen; and you can bet it was a challenge to identify them with no color clues at all!

In general, birders use four main clues to identify a bird: geography, shape and size, markings, and behavior. Geography eliminates many choices right away. If you live east of the Mississippi River, chances are, your hummingbird is a Ruby-throated. Although during migration season, and in winter, other species of hummingbirds may venture east of the Mississippi, particularly in the Gulf Coast states. Bird banders have found nine species in the East: Allen's, Anna's, Broad-tailed, Black-chinned, Buff-bellied, Calliope, Magnificent, Ruby-throated and Rufous.

In Alaska, Rufous Hummingbirds are the only possibility. In Canada, five species nest: Black-chinned, Ruby-throated, Calliope, Rufous and Anna's. In certain areas of Texas, New Mexico and Arizona, the identification becomes even more complex since many more species are frequently found.

A second consideration is shape and size. Magnificent Hummingbirds and Blue-throated Hummingbirds are so much bigger than the others, you can pick them out right away.

The third thing to look for is field marks—the stripes, dots, color patches, bill lengths and shapes—that can all add up to help you make an identification.

The fourth clue to identifying a bird is its behavior. An experienced naturalist, in fact, will often use behavior more than field marks, identifying a bird by the motion of its flight, or whir of its wings. A Black-chinned Hummingbird, for instance, almost constantly flicks its spread-out tail as it feeds.

When trying to identify a hummingbird, bill color and tail shape may help point you in the right direction or quickly eliminate a possibility. Most species of hummingbirds that regularly occur in North America have black bills. However, the Broad-billed, White-eared, Berylline, Buff-bellied and Violet-crowned have completely or partially red bills. Whereas female Black-chinned and Costa's hummingbirds may have slightly decurved bills, the bill of the Lucifer Hummingbird is noticeably decurved. Hummingbird species with a slight to heavy forked tail include the Black-chinned, Ruby-throated, Broad-billed, Buff-bellied and Lucifer.

These are only general guidelines and exceptions can occur. Also, in the field, it is not always possible to get a clear view of a hummingbird's tail. However, when the identity of a hummingbird is in question, a good, sharp color picture of its spread tail is often sufficient to make the call.

All the difficulties of hummingbird identification make it an enjoyable challenge—a skill to be learned and honed.

This chapter profiles the sixteen hummingbird species that are known to nest in North America. Ten additional species that have be sighted in the United States, or are speculated to occur, are also mentioned.

Ruby-throated Hummingbirds

SPECIES ACCOUNTS

The following hummingbird species are known to nest in North America. They are listed in alphabetical order according to their common names. Unless otherwise noted, all measurements are species averages for males and females. For each species, a range of body lengths and weights is given. In North American hummingbirds, the males and females of a species usually differ in size. In the smaller species, the females tend to be larger, whereas in the larger species, the females tend to be smaller than the males.

Information on field markings is limited; for more details, readers are advised to refer to a reliable field guide.

Anna's Hummingbird

ALLEN'S HUMMINGBIRD

Scientific name	*Selasphorus sasin*
Body length	2.99 to 3.5 in
Body weight	0.07 to 0.12 oz
Range	Central to northwestern Mexico; breeding range in U.S. along the coasts of California north to southern Oregon.
Breeding data	In the U.S., breeds from mid-February to early July. Nests in a variety of locales, from low in shrubs to high in trees.
Field marks	Very similar in appearance to Rufous except that adult males usually have almost entirely green backs; tail feathers are narrower than in Rufous.
Notes	Adult male's wing buzz similar to Rufous, but may be higher pitched. It is extremely difficult in the field to distinguish female and immature Allen's from female and immature Rufous Hummingbirds.

ANNA'S HUMMINGBIRD

Scientific name	*Calypte anna*
Body length	3.2 to 3.8 in
Body weight	0.13 to 0.15 oz
Range	Resident of Baja California, southern Arizona, to far western Texas (El Paso), coastal California, Oregon, Washington and southwestern British Columbia. May extend range in winter to the Texas coast.
Breeding data	Breeds December to June. Early breeding is limited to southern ranges. Often nests in oak trees in chaparral.
Field marks	Males have a rose-red head and slightly elongated rose-red gorget; females may have fine red spots on throat.
Notes	This is the only species in North America in which the entire population is resident. It is an altitudinal migrant, moving to higher altitudes to take advantage of the blooming season in the mountains.

BERYLLINE HUMMINGBIRD

Scientific name	*Amazilia beryllina*
Body length	3.54 to 3.81 in
Body weight	0.16 to 0.172 oz
Range	Northwest to central Mexican mountains with breeding range extending to the mountains of southeastern Arizona, in particular the Huachuca, Chiricahua and Santa Rita Mountains.
Breeding data	In the U.S., breeds in the mountains of southeastern Arizona, typically July through August. Most nests are located in Arizona sycamores in riparian habitat.
Field marks	Emerald-green underparts; black-tipped, red bill; rufous-purple colored wings; wide tail; sexes similar.
Notes	Of the breeding species in North America, the Berylline is the one least seen.

BLACK-CHINNED HUMMINGBIRD

Scientific name	*Archilochus alexandri*
Body length	2.91 to 3.66 in
Body weight	0.08 to 0.115 oz
Range	West-central Mexico and Baja California; breeding range in North America includes southwestern British Columbia, western Montana, south through California, Arizona, New Mexico and the western two-thirds of Texas.
Breeding data	In North America, breeds April through August. Average nest height is less than 9.84 ft, and is often placed in the fork of a small limb. Nests are usually not covered with lichen.
Field marks	Notched tail; slightly decurved bill; males have a black chin bordered below by a purple band; obvious white chest; dusky green flanks. Females have white throats and chests, green backs, and white-tipped tail feathers.
Notes	Females and immatures of Ruby-throated and Black-chinned may be confused with each other. A few individuals may over-winter in Texas, Arizona, and southern California. Males produce a dry wing buzz in flight.

BLUE-THROATED HUMMINGBIRD

Scientific name   *Lampornis clemenciae*

Body length   4.8 to 5.2 in

Body weight   0.25 to 0.33 oz

Range   Mountains of Mexico; breeding range in U.S. includes extreme southeastern Arizona, southwestern New Mexico, and southwestern Texas.

Breeding data   In the U.S., breeds from late April to July. Has been known to build nests fastened to plant stalks over or near water.

Field marks   Large size; both sexes have two white stripes on face, one above and one below the eyes; Long blackish tail with white patches on outside feathers; male has a light blue gorget.

Notes   The Blue-throated Hummingbird is North America's heaviest hummingbird. Individuals have been known to stray into Colorado after breeding season. Found in riparian habitat in mountain canyons.

BROAD-BILLED HUMMINGBIRD

Scientific name   *Cyanthus latirostris*

Body length   3.34 to 3.7 in

Body weight   0.105 to 0.127 oz

Range   Northwestern to south-central Mexico; breeding range in U.S. includes south-western Texas, southeastern Arizona and extreme southwestern New Mexico.

Breeding data   In the U.S., breeds from mid-April to August. Nests are usually built above a streambed or a dry wash (arroyo).

Field marks   Bright red bill with black tip; dark, forked tail; male has metallic green body with bluish throat; female has metallic green upperparts and grayish underparts.

Notes   Some reports indicate that Broad-billeds nesting above arroyos typically build nests that resemble the clumps of plant material that get trapped in shrubs during floods.

BROAD-TAILED HUMMINGBIRD

Scientific name   *Selasphorus platycercus*

Body length   3.26 to 3.81 in

Body weight   0.112 to 0.15 oz

Range   Mountains of Mexico down to Guatemala; breeding range in U.S. includes the mountains of eastern California, northern Wyoming, south through the Rocky Mountains and Great Basin ranges to southern Arizona, New Mexico, and western Texas.

Breeding data   In U.S., breeds from March to July. Some accounts mention that Broad-taileds nest in the same location year after year, building a new nest on top of the old one.

Field marks   Broad, greenish tail; male has green crown, rose-red gorget, and greenish sides; female has cinnamon wash on sides, and some spotting on throat.

Notes   In flight, notched tip of adult males' outermost primaries produces a loud, musical trill. This species is a high altitude nester often enduring chilly nighttime temperatures. A few regularly overwinter in southeastern Arizona, the Texas Gulf Coast, and occasionally along the upper Gulf Coast.

BUFF-BELLIED HUMMINGBIRD
(FORMERLY CALLED FAWN-BREASTED HUMMINGBIRD)

Scientific name	*Amazilia yucatanensis*
Body length	3.6 to 4.25 in
Body weight	0.12 to 0.14 oz
Range	Gulf Coast of Mexico, Belize and Guatemala with breeding range extending to extreme southeastern Texas.
Breeding data	In the U.S, breeds March through July. Nests are usually found in small trees and bushes in dense vegetation.
Field marks	Black-tipped red bill; forked tail rufous in color; head and upperparts emerald-green; belly pale buff to gray; sexes similar.
Notes	Winters in Mexico, but some overwinter in Texas with a few occasionally spreading out along the Texas and Louisiana coast.

CALLIOPE HUMMINGBIRD

Scientific name   *Stellula calliope*

Body length   2.75 to 3.2 in

Body weight   0.07 to 0.126 oz

Range   Central to northwestern Mexico; breeding range in North America includes mountains of central British Columbia, southwestern Alberta, Washington, Idaho, western Montana, northwestern Wyoming, eastern Oregon, northeastern to central California and Nevada.

Breeding data   In North America, breeds mid-May through July. Nests at high elevations. Nests are often positioned to take advantage of early morning sun.

Field marks   Very small size; short bill; male's magenta-red gorget is divided into separate rays; females often have dusky spots on throat.

Notes   This is the smallest breeding bird in North America. Adult males can raise the gorget feathers, which stand out against the white background of the throat. This creates what has been described as a star-burst display.

COSTA'S HUMMINGBIRD

Scientific name	*Calypte costae*
Body length	2.95 to 3.4 in
Body weight	0.07 to 0.134 oz
Range	Resident populations in Baja California, extreme northwestern Mexico, southeastern California, and southwestern Arizona. Breeding range extends farther into California, Arizona and Nevada.
Breeding data	Breeds from mid-February through June. Nests typically are built at edges of tall shrubs or, in desert regions, in cacti and dead yucca stalks.
Field marks	Bill relatively short; males have a deep violet-blue head and elongated violet-blue gorget; with age females develop spotting on throat.
Notes	Costa's Hummingbirds prefer the driest climates of all North American hummingbird species. Nests are typically located far away from water.

LUCIFER HUMMINGBIRD

Scientific name *Calothorax lucifer*

Body length 3.2 to 3.6 in

Body weight 0.098 to 0.134 oz

Range Central to northern Mexico; breeding range in U.S. includes extreme southwestern Texas, southwestern New Mexico and southeastern Arizona. Usually found in arid mesas and foothills.

Breeding data In the U.S., breeds from April to August. In Texas, nests are often located in agaves, cholla cacti and ocotillos.

Field marks Decurved bill; deeply forked tail; male has long violet gorget. Female lacks forked tail.

Notes Female Lucifers may be confused with female Costa's or Black-chinneds, which have slightly decurved bills.

MAGNIFICENT HUMMINGBIRD

(FORMERLY CALLED RIVOLI'S HUMMINGBIRD)

Scientific name   *Eugenes fulgens*

Body length   4.68 to 5.35 in

Body weight   0.249 to 0.352 oz

Range   Mountains of Mexico down to Panama; breeding range in U.S. includes extreme southeastern Arizona and southwestern New Mexico, and Chisos and Guadalupe mountains of Texas.

Breeding data   In the U.S., breeds from May to July. Nest usually placed on a horizontal limb.

Field marks   Large size; has a long bill and flat forehead; female rather plain with white eye stripe, grayish underparts; male has purple crown and bright green throat contrasting with dark underparts.

Notes   A few individuals may overwinter in Arizona, taking advantage of feeders. It is a casual wanderer to Colorado. It has been sighted in Nevada and Utah. Typically occurs at or above 4,900 ft in coniferous forest and riparian habitat.

RUBY-THROATED HUMMINGBIRD

Scientific name   *Archilochus colubris*

Body length   3.07 to 3.66 in

Body weight   0.088 to 0.112 oz

Range   Southern Mexico to Central America; breeding range in North America includes central Alberta to Nova Scotia, and south through the eastern Great Plains, east to the Atlantic, and south to all the Gulf Coast states.

Breeding data   In North America, breeds from late March to August. Nests are almost always sheltered from above by a limb and usually located above a brook or open area.

Field marks   Males have forked tail; underparts are whitish; dusky green flanks; males have a ruby-red gorget. Females are whitish on chin and underparts.

Notes   This is the only hummingbird regularly occurring in the East. Females and immatures of Ruby-throated and Black-chinned may be confused with each other. One study in Michigan reported several females that relied almost exclusively on tree sap during the nesting season; they were rarely seen visiting flowers.

RUFOUS HUMMINGBIRD

Scientific name	*Selasphorus rufus*
Body length	2.87 to 3.58 in
Body weight	0.097 to 0.141 oz
Range	Mexico; breeding range in North America includes southeastern Alaska, southern Yukon, British Columbia, southwestern Alberta, western Montana to Washington and northern California.
Breeding data	In North America, breeds from April to July. One study found that to minimize temperature fluctuations, springtime nests were often located low in conifers, before deciduous trees leafed out. In summer, the nests were located in deciduous canopies, protected from the sun.
Field marks	Tail mainly rufous colored; males have rufous upperparts flecked with green, and orange-red gorget; females have rufous sides and small red to golden-green spots on throat.
Notes	It is extremely difficult in the field to distinguish female and immature Rufous Hummingbirds from female and immature Allen's. In flight, males produce a high-pitched trill, quieter than a Broad-tailed's. A few individuals often travel to the East after breeding season. Some overwinter along the Gulf Coast states.

VIOLET-CROWNED HUMMINGBIRD

Scientific name   *Amazilia violiceps*

Body length   3.78 to 4.25 in

Body weight   0.186 to 0.208 oz

Range   Western to southern Mexico with breeding
                   range extending to the extreme
                   southeastern corner of Arizona and
                   southwestern New Mexico.

Breeding data   In the U.S., typically breeds June through
                   August. Nests are usually found in Arizona
                   sycamores in riparian habitats from low to
                   middle canyon elevations.

Field marks   Violet-blue crown; black-tipped red bill;
                   underparts entirely white; sexes similar.

Notes   There have been a few reported sightings
                   of Violet-crowneds in southern California.
                   Also, a few individuals have overwintered
                   in Arizona.

WHITE-EARED HUMMINGBIRD

Scientific name   *Hylocharis leucotis*

Body length   3.34 to 3.93 in

Body weight   0.116 to 0.137 oz

Range   Mountains of Mexico down to Nicaragua;
                  breeding range in U.S. includes south-
                  eastern Arizona.

Breeding data   In U.S., breeds June to April. Nests are
                  often found in shrubs and small trees.

Field marks   Black-tipped red bill; noticeable white line
                  behind eye; male has violet-blue crown,
                  purplish forehead and chin, and green
                  gorget; females have green spots on throat
                  and sometimes appear to have greenish
                  barred sides. Both sexes almost always have
                  a blackish ear patch.

Notes   Many reports of this rare breeder in
                  Arizona are often attributed to misidenti-
                  fied female or immature Broad-billeds.
                  This species is a bird of higher elevations.
                  Has been seen in the Chisos Mountains of
                  Texas, and the Animas Mountains of New
                  Mexico.

Visitors

In addition to the sixteen species of hummingbirds that breed in North America, ten additional species have visited the United States. As visitors, these species fall into the category of rare (occurs in very small numbers each year), to casual (occurs in very small numbers but not annually), to accidental (only a few records of a species far outside its normal range).

When a sighting is confirmed, news spreads quickly among the birding community via various birding hotlines. Many birders who maintain lists of bird species they have seen make special trips at a moment's notice to see such a rare bird, hoping to check off another species on their life list. A few of these species are not yet officially accepted as occurring in North America; the status of some is being reconsidered. One species is hypothetical as there is only one record of its appearance in Texas.

Antillean Crested (*Orthorhyncus cristatus*): This species is currently treated as hypothetical since only one badly damaged specimen exists. The bird in question was apparently netted on February 1, 1967, by two boys on Galveston Island, Texas. It was later turned over to a man who then reported it to a local ornithologist. Even though parts of the bird were missing, it was identified as an Antillean Crested Hummingbird. However, because the bird was far from its normal range of Puerto Rico, the Virgin Islands and the Lesser Antilles, and due to the circumstances of its capture, many questions still remain. Some speculate that the bird had been captured in its home range and later transported to the island where it escaped or was released.

Bahama Woodstar (*Calliphlox evelynae*): This species is considered accidental in southern Florida. Its normal range encompasses most of the Bahama Islands. It is a dull green-backed bird with a cinnamon-gray belly and white breast. It has a deeply forked, rufous- and black-colored tail. The male's gorget is metallic purple and red. The first specimen of this species in North America was found on January 31, 1961, in Miami. The bird was dead, its bill stuck in a window screen. A second bird was sighted in 1971 over the period of August 26 to October 13 in Lantana, Florida. A third record came from Homestead, Florida where a molting immature male was seen from April 7 to June 1, 1974.

Bumblebee (*Atthis heloisa*): This is considered an accidental species. Only two records of its occurrence in the U.S. exist. On July 2, 1896, two female hummingbirds of this species were collected in the Huachuca Mountains in Ramsey Canyon. For almost one hundred years, no other sightings have been reported. However, the identity of these two specimens is recently being questioned. It is a very small hummingbird, similar in appearance to the Calliope. It lives only in Mexico and specimens there have not been collected closer than a hundred miles from the U.S. border.

Cinnamon (*Amazilia rutila*): This species is an accidental visitor with only two records in North America. This green-backed species has a black-tipped, red bill, buffy to rufous colored underparts and a rufous-colored tail. It is a resident of Mexico and Central America. The first fully-confirmed sighting was in Patagonia, Arizona, July 21 to 23, 1992. A second sighting was in Santa Theresa, New Mexico.

Cuban Emerald (*Chlorostilbon ricordii*): This bird species is casual in the fall and winter in southern Florida. It is a West Indian bird, residing in Cuba, the northern Bahamas and the Isle of Pines. The male of this species is almost entirely iridescent green. The female is green-backed but grayish below. This species has a deeply forked tail and its lower mandible is often pinkish in hue. There have been a handful of sightings of this species in and around southern Florida.

Green Violet-ear (*Colibri thalassinus*): This rare-to-casual species, named for the violet patch on its ear, is usually seen in southern or central Texas. Its normal range includes the highlands of Mexico to Bolivia. It is an all-green bird with a bluish tail and usually a small blue to violet spot on the chest. Sexes are similar. In recent years, this species has been seen each year in Texas. In late October of 1995, one was trapped in a mist net in Mobile, Alabama.

Green-breasted Mango (*Anthracothorax prevostii*): This is an accidental species. This relatively large green-backed hummingbird is normally a resident of northeastern Mexico to central Panama. Its bill is noticeably decurved. This species is thought to have been seen in Brownsville, Texas, in 1988. But not until January of 1992 was the North American occurrence of this species verified. At a feeder in Corpus Christi, Texas, January 6 to 27, 1992, an immature or female Green-breasted Mango was seen regularly. The bird was photographed, trapped and banded to fully document its appearance. Another report for this species came from the Santa Ana National Wildlife Refuge in Texas.

Plain-capped Starthroat (*Heliomaster constantii*): This species is considered casual in summer and fall in the foothills of southeastern Arizona. This relatively large hummingbird normally ranges from western Mexico to Costa Rica. It is a long-billed species, with broad white eye stripes, a white streak on the rump, and a red gorget bordered by white whisker stripes. A handful of sightings have been reported in Arizona with the most recent report in late August, 1995, in the famous Sierra Vista Sewage Lagoons. Some, however, are found each year in the Chiricahua Mountains.

Rufous-tailed (*Amazilia tzacatl*): This species is considered accidental in southern Texas. It is similar in appearance to the Buff-bellied Hummingbird except that it does not have a forked tail and its abdomen is brownish-gray instead of buff colored. Its normal range includes eastern Mexico to western Ecuador. Only two verified records came from Fort Brown, Texas, in June and July of 1876. Two additional unauthenticated sightings occurred on November 11 to 12, 1969, in LaPorte, Texas and August 20, 1975 in Brownsville, Texas. However, it is still not an accepted species on some checklists.

Xantus' (*Hylocharis xantusii*): This is an accidental species with one authenticated record of a nesting female found in Ventura, California, in 1988. Many people saw and photographed the bird. However, its nesting attempt was unsuccessful. Its normal range is in Baja California.

Hybrids

As mentioned earlier, hummingbirds exhibit a higher than usual frequency of interbreeding, or hybridizing. A hybrid is the offspring of two different species. One possible reason hybridization is more common in hummingbirds is that there is no strong pair bond formed between mated individuals. Also, the males frequently mate with more than one female and are often seen chasing females of different hummingbird species.

Below is a list of known hybrids. Some of the combinations occur with relative frequency; others are known to have occurred once or possibly a few times. Because identifying hybrids can be very difficult, especially with certain hummingbird combinations, it is more than likely that this list is incomplete.

Anna's x Allen's

Anna's x Black-chinned

Anna's x Costa's

Black-chinned x Broad-tailed

Black-chinned x Costa's

Blue-throated x Anna's

Blue-throated x Black-chinned

Broad-tailed x Costa's

Calliope x Anna's

Calliope x Costa's

Calliope x Rufous

Magnificent x Blue-throated

Magnificent x Violet-crowned

Rufous x Allen's

White-eared x Broad-tailed

Following page: Anna's Hummingbird

SELECTED RESOURCES

Hummingbird Books

Grant, K. A. and V. Grant. *Hummingbirds and Their Flowers.* New York: Columbia University Press, 1968.

Greenwalt, C. H. *Hummingbirds.* Garden City: Doubleday & Co., 1960.

Holmgren, Virginia. *The Way of the Hummingbird.* Santa Barbara: Capra Press, 1986.

Johnsgard, Paul A. *The Hummingbirds of North America.* Washington, D.C.: Smithsonian Institute Press, 1983.

Lazaroff, David Wentworth. *The Secret Lives of Hummingbirds.* Arizona–Sonora Desert Museum, 1995.

Skutch, Alexander F. *The Life of the Hummingbird.* New York: Crown Publishers, 1973.

Stokes, Donald and Lillian Stokes. *The Hummingbird Book.* Boston: Little, Brown and Co., 1989.

Hummingbird-Related Festivals

Hummer / Bird Celebration
Rockport–Fullerton Area Chamber of Commerce
404 Broadway
Rockport, TX 78382
This four-day festival in early September features lectures and workshops on hummingbirds, hummingbird gardening and related topics. Some field trips and banding demonstrations.

Southwest Wings Birding Festival
P.O. Box 3432
Sierra Vista, AZ 85636
This four-day festival in August generally includes hummingbird lectures, banding demonstrations, and visits to hummingbird hotspots such as Ramsey Canyon, Patagonia–Sonoita Creek and Rustler Park.

Non-Profit Organizations

Friends of the San Pedro River
1763 Paseo San Luis
Sierra Vista, AZ 85635-4611
    This organization has education programs, habitat restoration efforts and hummingbird banding.

The Hummer / Bird Study Group, Inc.
P.O. Box 250
Clay, AL 35048-2888
    This small, non-profit group funds banding and educational programs.

National Fish and Wildlife Foundation
1120 Connecticut Avenue NW
Suite 900
Washington, DC 20036
    This organization coordinates Partners in Flight, a program of cooperative efforts to conserve habitat used by migratory birds in North America, Central America, South America and the Caribbean.

Ramsey Canyon Preserve
27 Ramsey Canyon Road
Hereford, AZ 85615
    Ramsey Canyon is a Nature Conservancy property.